DEREK PRINCE

ULTIMATE SECURITY

WHITAKER
HOUSE

ULTIMATE SECURITY:
Finding a Refuge in Difficult Times

Derek Prince Ministries–International
P.O. Box 19501
Charlotte, North Carolina 28219-9501
www.derekprince.org

ISBN: 978-1-62911-166-7 • eBook ISBN: 978-1-62911-167-4
Printed in the United States of America
© 2014 by Derek Prince Ministries–International

Whitaker House
1030 Hunt Valley Circle
New Kensington, PA 15068
www.whitakerhouse.com

Library of Congress Cataloging-in-Publication Data

Prince, Derek.
  Ultimate security : finding a refuge in difficult times / Derek Prince.
    pages cm
  Summary: "Addressing the universal question 'Where can I find true security?' author Derek Prince points readers to the Source that can give them total and permanent security—in this life and for eternity" —Provided by publisher.
  ISBN 978-1-62911-166-7 (trade pbk. : alk. paper) — ISBN 978-1-62911-167-4 (ebook) 1. Salvation—Christianity. 2. Faith. 3. Assurance (Theology) I. Title.
  BT751.3.P75 2014
  234—dc23

1 2 3 4 5 6 7 8 9 10 11 **LU** 21 20 19 18 17 16 15 14

CONTENTS

INTRODUCTION

SECURITY—A BASIC HUMAN CONCERN

Where can I find security? People everywhere ask themselves this question—regardless of their nationality, culture, or socioeconomic status. The languages they use to express the question vary. But the question of where to find security is the same for all people. We all are concerned with obtaining security. It is a universal quest. In fact, a major part of human activity is directed toward this end.

Security Agencies

One way to estimate the importance people attach to a pursuit is to measure how much they are willing to spend for it. In our contemporary culture, there are numerous agencies, industries, and organizations devoted in some way to providing security—involving the expenditure of countless billions of dollars every year.

Let's consider just a few such agencies and organizations. First, there are insurance companies. They do a tremendous job, but their scope is limited. You can insure yourself against an accident, but there is no way to ensure that an accident will not happen. You can insure your home or business against fire and theft, but there is no way to be completely certain a fire will not break out or a theft will not take place. So, insurance companies can guarantee some protections against adverse circumstances, but other situations remain outside their control.

Then there are both public and private security agencies. Public security forces include national, state, and local law enforcement officers. As we all know, a whole new industry has arisen for providing security in airports. Also, there are countless private security agencies whose numbers are multiplying every year. Yet, in spite of the fine work of many of these agencies, it is a sad fact that crimes of violence and acts of terrorism continue to increase. This is not a criticism of these agencies, but rather a confirmation that there are limits to what security agencies can achieve.

Security Forces

Another type of security in our world today is represented by the armed forces of a nation, ═such as the army, the navy, and the air force. Every country claims to maintain its armed forces for its own security. In many cases, this is probably true. However, these forces do not provide total security.

For example, consider the military forces of the United States and the Soviet Union during the Cold War years. The stronger the security forces of the Soviet Union, the greater the insecurity of the American people. And the stronger the security forces of the United States, the greater the insecurity of the Soviet people. It is a simple equation: What constitutes security for one nation may automatically be a source of insecurity for another nation.

Social Security

There is also what we call "social security." Under this term, I include various governmental programs that have collectively become a major element in the life of nearly all Western nations.

This "cradle-to-grave security" is a system by which resources for every major need arising in the life of a normal person will be provided by his government. If he gets sick, his medical expenses, including any hospitalization costs, will be covered. When he becomes too old and weak to work, he will receive an income to cover his needs. Unfortunately, shaky economic conditions are already deflating some of the claims of "social security."

Interestingly enough, various nations have achieved a very high degree of efficiency in their social-security systems. Two examples are Sweden and Denmark, which have marvelous social-security programs. Unfortunately, the provisions of those systems are matched by extremely high taxes.

It is also interesting to note that, even in the earlier years of the provision of such security, Sweden and Denmark were statistically ranked as two of the nations with the highest suicide rate in the world. What does that fact indicate? That even social security does not provide total security. Here were people who theoretically had all their obvious physical and financial needs cared for. Yet these same people somehow could not face life; rather, they opted for the alternative of suicide. Again, this is evidence that there is no such thing as "complete security" based on social programs.

Is Total Security Possible?

Many of the above entities that attempt to provide security are very worthwhile. They are to be commended and supported. However, none of them has achieved—nor can it achieve—either total or permanent security. Not only are there many areas in which those entities cannot provide security, but even in those areas in which they can provide a modicum of security, the scope of that security is limited by time and circumstances.

Therefore, since a basic drive of human existence is to seek security, it seems important to consider this question: *Where can I find **true** security?* In considering that question, I have come to one striking conclusion: In spite of all man's efforts and expenditures, he is ultimately powerless to achieve true security. Furthermore, I believe that the only hope of achieving real security is to admit this conclusion from the start—to face the fact that any man-made agency is ultimately powerless to bring security.

If that indeed is the case, we cannot build our lives and our hopes on any entity that provides only the illusion of real security. But there is a Source that can provide us with total and permanent security. That Source is the focus of this book, *Ultimate Security: Finding a Refuge in Difficult Times*.

1

THE TRUE SOURCE

Having accepted the conclusion of the introduction to this book—that no human agency can provide anything other than an illusion of real security—where do we turn? Thankfully, there is another Source of security—one that is completely different in its nature and in the type of security it offers. This alternative can provide both total and permanent security. What is this Source? It is God, in whom are found all wisdom and provision.

As we begin to explore the nature of God's wisdom, let us consider a passage from Proverbs 1 in which wisdom is personified. As you read this passage, notice carefully the alternatives that are presented: the instability of human achievement versus the total security God offers. Please notice, also, that it is not human wisdom talking here; rather, the wisdom of God is speaking through the Scriptures.

Wisdom calls aloud in the street, she raises her voice in the public squares; at the head of the noisy streets she cries out, in the gateways of the city she makes her speech: "How long will you simple ones love your simple ways? How long will mockers delight in mockery and fools hate knowledge? If you had responded to my rebuke, I would have poured out my heart to you and made my thoughts known to you. But since you rejected me when I called and no one gave heed when I stretched out my hand, since you ignored all my advice and would not accept my rebuke, I in turn will laugh at your disaster; I will mock when calamity overtakes you—when calamity overtakes you like a storm, when disaster sweeps over you like a whirlwind, when distress and troubles over-whelm you. Then they will call to me but I will not answer; they will look for me but will not find me. Since they hated knowledge and did not choose to fear the LORD, since they would not accept my advice and spurned my rebuke, they will eat the fruit of their ways and be filled with the fruit of their schemes. For the waywardness of the simple will kill them, and the complacency of fools will destroy them; but whoever listens to me will live in safety and be at ease, without fear of harm."

(Proverbs 1:20–33)

Please ponder that last sentence with me: *"But whoever listens to me will live in safety and be at ease, without fear of harm."* That is total security—the offer of God's wisdom speaking to us through the pages of Scripture.

We should note that even though Wisdom makes this offer to everyone, there are few who accept it. This passage specifically indicates that there are many who are unwilling to receive Wisdom's instruction and heed her rebuke. Consequently, they are headed for a calamity they could have avoided.

The question each of us must answer is this: Am I prepared to listen and give heed to the voice of Wisdom? Will I give myself to God's wisdom, the only source that promises me total and permanent security?

2

THE CHOICE WE FACE

According to the passage from Proverbs we examined in chapter 1, Wisdom's offer of security is so complete that the person who receives it will not only *"live in safety"* but also *"be at ease."* That person will have no fear. He or she will be outside the scope of all harm! (See Proverbs 1:33.)

However, it is clear that Wisdom's offer is for both advice *and* rebuke. (See Proverbs 1:23.) Alas, the majority of people will not avail themselves of the advice and will not heed the rebuke. Therefore, Wisdom says,

> *Since you ignored all my advice and would not accept my rebuke, I in turn will laugh at your disaster; I will mock when calamity overtakes you....* (Proverbs 1:25–26)

This is the grim alternative to accepting Wisdom's advice and heeding Wisdom's rebuke: ultimate disaster and calamity. Therefore, we are left with a choice—either to live safely without fear or to face calamity. The result we experience will depend on whether we heed the voice of Wisdom.

In offering both advice and rebuke, Wisdom not only shows us what is right, but also warns us about what is wrong. Of special interest to us is an aspect of the wisdom of God that cannot be understood apart from God's revelation in the Scriptures. This is the distinction between two categories in the universe: *what is temporal* and *what is eternal.* Unless we come to see this distinction and act upon it, we can never achieve true, enduring security.

The Temporal Versus the Eternal

In his second letter to the Corinthians, Paul wrote about these two categories, or realms:

> *So we fix our eyes not on what is seen, but on what is unseen.*
> *For what is seen is temporary, but what is unseen is eternal.*
>
> (2 Corinthians 4:18)

In this verse, Paul makes a very clear distinction between these two categories. First, there is the "seen" material world that we can experience through our physical senses. Such material realities are temporary; they do not endure. Second, there is the unseen eternal world—the world of God, the world of His being and His truth. This eternal, invisible world is completely distinct from the temporal world that we can see; it endures forever.

Paul said, *"We fix our eyes…on what is unseen."* This is an amazing paradox. How can you look at what you cannot see? Here is the answer to that life-shaping question: The only way you can enter into the realm of the unseen is through faith. By faith, we apprehend what we cannot see with our physical eyes and what we cannot perceive with any of our other physical senses. Through our perception of this eternal, invisible realm, we begin to find true security.

In similar fashion to Paul's teaching, the prophet Isaiah declared very vividly the distinction between the temporal and the eternal. He showed us that, through the temporal, God draws us toward the eternal.

> *All men are like grass, and all their glory is like the flowers*
> *of the field. The grass withers and the flowers fall, because the*

breath of the LORD *blows on them. Surely the people are grass.
The grass withers and the flowers fall, but the word of our God
stands forever.*   (Isaiah 40:6–8)

Like Paul, Isaiah makes a clear distinction between the temporal and the eternal. All human life is temporal. All of us are just like grass: we grow up, we wither, we die, and we pass away. There is nothing permanent in all of human existence. Yet, like the flowers, the temporal realm can be very beautiful. Through that beauty, God is attracting us to the eternal. He is speaking to us about another realm where beauty never fades and where the flowers do not wither; a realm that is not subject to corruption, change, instability, and insecurity. This is the eternal realm revealed by the Word of God, and Isaiah summarizes the contrast: *"The grass withers and the flowers fall, but the word of our God stands forever."*

---

*Through the beauty of the temporal realm,
God is attracting us to the eternal.*

A True Foundation

As I have pointed out, in order to attain true security, we must recognize the limitations of any other kind of security. We must come to grips with the fact that any security human beings may achieve by their own efforts or wisdom can never be permanent. This is true because humanity's own nature is impermanent. Human life grows up like the grass of the fields—it is vivid, green, and beautiful with its flowers; but just when it reaches its climax of beauty, it begins to wither.

God has permitted this demonstration of reality in nature to turn our hearts away from the impermanent and toward the permanent. He desires to move us from what is temporary to what endures. Hopefully, this recognition on our part will turn us to God, to His Word, and to His wisdom. He speaks to us from His Word and offers us a different kind of security—one that is total and permanent.

Confronted by this contrast between the temporary and the permanent, you and I must make a choice about our lives. We must decide whether we are going to build on what is temporary or on what is permanent.

The contrast in this choice is clearly illustrated by Jesus' familiar parable about two men who each built a house. One man built on sand, which was temporary; the other built on rock, which was permanent. Jesus said,

> *Therefore everyone who hears these words of mine and puts them into practice is like a wise man who built his house on the rock. The rain came down, the streams rose, and the winds blew and beat against that house; yet it did not fall, because it had its foundation on the rock. But everyone who hears these words of mine and does not put them into practice is like a foolish man who built his house on sand. The rain came down, the streams rose, and the winds blew and beat against that house, and it fell with a great crash.*   (Matthew 7:24–27)

Jesus presents such a clear choice—with no halfway in between and no way for compromise. You and I must decide how we are going to build—what the foundation of our lives will be. Are we going to be satisfied with the temporary? Will we restrict ourselves to the inadequate security we might assemble by our own efforts? If you and I depend upon the security of the temporal realm, we are like the man who built his house on sand, without an adequate foundation. That house will stand for a time. But, when the tests, calamities, and pressures of life come, it will collapse.

Please note that Jesus was very realistic. He did not say, "*If* the tests come...." He said, in effect, "*When* the tests come...." Here is the plain truth as Jesus spoke it: Tests *will* come. Every life will be tested at some point by all kinds of pressure. We cannot hope to escape these pressures. The only solution is to build on a foundation that will endure the pressures that will inevitably come, without yielding to them.

As Jesus clearly stated in His parable, that foundation is the Word of God and the wisdom revealed therein. God's wisdom reveals His eternal nature, contains His eternal counsel, and shows us the way through the shifting sands of time to the Rock that is eternal—the Rock upon which we can all build with absolute confidence. We know that foundation can withstand all the pressures that life may bring against it. Is that the Rock you have chosen to build upon in your quest for security?

---

*We must decide on what foundation
we will build our lives.*

3

THE ETERNAL ROCK

In this chapter, we will expand upon our consideration of the nature of the eternal Rock. It is the Rock alone upon which we can build with total security, both for time and for eternity. There is no secret about the identity of this Rock—it is clearly unfolded to us in the Bible. In 1 Corinthians 3:11, Paul wrote, *"For no one can lay any foundation other than the one already laid, which is Jesus Christ."*

Paul's statement is very clear and very practical: The only foundation that will stand for eternity is the foundation of Jesus Christ. Our Lord and Savior is the foundation God has already laid. We cannot change this simple truth, nor we can we find another foundation God will accept. We can rely solely upon the foundation that God has provided for us in Jesus Christ.

Concerning our Foundation, the apostle Peter wrote,

As you come to [Jesus], the living Stone—rejected by men but chosen by God and precious to him—you also, like living stones, are being built into a spiritual house to be a holy priesthood, offering spiritual sacrifices acceptable to God through Jesus Christ. For in Scripture it says: "See, I lay a stone in Zion, a chosen and precious cornerstone, and the one who trusts in him will never be put to shame." (1 Peter 2:4–6)

Similar to Paul's statement, Peter presented Jesus as *"the living Stone,"* the *"chosen and precious cornerstone."* Furthermore, Peter explained that if we will come to Jesus and put our trust in Him, we will become *"living stones,…built into a spiritual house"* upon the foundation that is Christ. That *"spiritual house"* will provide us with total security. Notice that Peter said the one who trusts in Jesus *"will never be put to shame."* The word *"never"* covers both time and eternity. The one who trusts that Foundation will never be disappointed, never be let down, and never be confronted with some situation for which Jesus cannot make provision.

Steps to Building on the Eternal Rock

There are two very simple but very important steps to building on this foundation of Jesus Christ:

1. You must renounce confidence in the temporal, in anything temporary, in all human effort, in all human wisdom, and in yourself. In the last resort, they are all "sand." (See Matthew 7:26–27.) You must renounce them.

2. You must make a total, unreserved commitment of yourself and your life—all that you are and all that you have, for time and eternity—to Jesus Christ.

You may already be a religious, moral person who "lives a good life." In the last resort, however, the best you can offer is just "sand"—mere human effort. To build on the Rock, you must renounce your own self-righteousness, goodness, and morality as a basis for permanent security and come to Jesus for that security.

Jesus Himself has given us the following promise: *"Whoever comes to me I will never drive away* ["reject" TLB]*"* (John 6:37). If you come to Him, He will receive you. If you realize that you have been building on your own foundation, you can come to Jesus right now by simply praying the following:

Jesus, I come to You. I trust You to be my Savior. By faith, I receive from You the gift of eternal life. Right now, I put my life wholly and unreservedly in Your hands. Amen.

These two simple but life-changing steps are the way you begin to build on the eternal Rock, Jesus Christ.

A Personal Relationship with Christ

Commitment to Jesus Christ produces a direct and personal relationship with Him for which there is no substitute. This relationship is described in many passages of Scripture. One of the most meaningful and familiar of these is Psalm 23, "The Shepherd's Psalm," written by King David. The first four verses beautifully unfold the nature of this relationship:

> *The LORD is my shepherd, I shall lack nothing. He makes me lie down in green pastures, he leads me beside quiet waters, he restores my soul. He guides me in paths of righteousness for his name's sake. Even though I walk through the valley of the shadow of death, I will fear no evil, for you are with me; your rod and your staff, they comfort me.*   (Psalm 23:1–4)

The first verse expresses everything that needs to be said about security, and it is based upon a personal relationship with the Lord: "*The LORD is my shepherd, I shall lack nothing.*" Everything I will ever need in time or eternity will be supplied out of that relationship. David continued, "*The LORD...makes me lie down in green pastures, he leads me beside quiet waters, he restores my soul. He guides me in paths of righteousness for his name's sake.*"

In essence, once we make a commitment to the Lord, God accepts total responsibility for us in every situation and circumstance "*for his name's sake.*" He does not do it because of our goodness or because we deserve His care. He gives us total security because He is faithful to His name. For the glory and honor of His name, He will keep His covenant and His commitment to us.

In the fourth verse, David goes on to say, *"Even though I walk through the valley of the shadow of death, I will fear no evil, for you are with me; your rod and your staff, they comfort me."* These words express a security that goes beyond time and into eternity. When our time comes—and it must come for each of us—we will say farewell to the temporal world and step out of it. When we do, we will not need to fear any evil. Even in the *"valley of the shadow of death"* the Lord is with us. He is there to uphold us, to strengthen us, to comfort us, and to receive us.

When we make a commitment to the Lord, God accepts total responsibility for us—in every situation and circumstance.

As a minister, the responsibility I often faced with people whose time had come was to bring them as far as I could—right to the entrance of the valley of the shadow. That would be the point when I, as a human minister, would then hand over to the eternal Good Shepherd the one whose life had been committed to Him and watch Him take responsibility for it. I had this experience with my first wife, Lydia, a beautiful Christian and a faithful servant of the Lord. I was by her side when she died, and I led her right to the entrance of the valley. Then, at a certain point, I could do no more, and the Lord was faithful to His commitment as she went peacefully into His presence. The Lord will do the same for everyone who makes that unreserved commitment to Him. He is faithful in life, faithful in death, faithful for time, and faithful for eternity. There is no evil power in the universe that can disrupt the relationship between the Lord and the one who is committed to Him.

Paul expressed this idea so eloquently:

For I am convinced that neither death nor life, neither angels nor demons, neither the present nor the future, nor any powers, neither height nor depth, nor anything else in all creation, will be able to separate us from the love of God that is in Christ Jesus our Lord. (Romans 8:38–39)

There is nothing in the whole created universe that can break the sacred relationship between the Lord and the soul who has turned to Jesus—the life that has been built on the eternal Rock, which is the Lord Jesus Christ. Above all else, such a foundation provides true, total, and permanent security.

4

"IN THE BEGINNING GOD…"

Having seen that true and permanent security is to be found only in a relationship with Jesus Christ, it will be helpful for us now to review *how* we have been brought into Christ as part of God's sovereign plan for each of us. Through the Scriptures, we will come to understand that we are totally secure in God's choice.

I invite you to join me on a wonderful journey that starts in eternity, leads us through the various phases of time, and takes us on again into eternity. If you will follow me in the path by which I will be leading you in this chapter, it will bring you to a place of total security in God.

We will begin our journey at the first verse of the Bible: *"In the beginning God created the heavens and the earth"* (Genesis 1:1). For virtually all of recorded history, human beings have speculated about what is behind the created universe and what keeps it going. Many different answers have been offered. Some philosophers have used the phrase "the first cause," knowing that something must be behind the origin of all creation. Is it chance? Is it a "big bang," as some physicists suggest? Is it a mindless physical process—one of which nobody knows the origin, or why it continues spontaneously, or how it will end? Is the universe something totally impossible to understand or to explain?

Our Creator-Father Gives Us Purpose

The Bible's answer to these questions is very clear and precise. It declares that behind the universe, there is a personal Creator who is also a Father. Three important concepts are included in that statement. Behind the universe is a *Person*. That Person is a *Creator*. Additionally, that Person is a *Father*.

The fact that the Creator is also a Father is extremely important. Why? Because your view of the origin of the universe will determine your perspective on yourself and your life. If you believe that your life is just a chance happening—that your existence is unexplainable, that you are merely a victim of inexorable physical forces that you cannot control but that control you—then what is the reason for your being here?

However, if you believe the record of the Bible, then behind everything that happens, there is a Creator. Even more, He is a Person to whom you can relate as a person. Further, not only is He a Person, but He is also a Father. If these statements are true, then you have a reason and a purpose for existing. That knowledge will change your whole outlook on life.

A minister friend once related the following experience to me. He had been ministering at a meeting in the inner city of a very large American metropolis. The meeting ended about dusk. It was a cold, windy evening, and he was alone on the sidewalk in a very gray, drab, cheerless, and unappealing situation. In those dark, oppressive surroundings, he felt extremely lonely, discouraged, and depressed. Then a thought came to him, and he began to whisper one word over and over again: "Father...Father...Father...Father."

For several minutes, he said the word "Father," and nothing else but that one word. As he persisted, his whole attitude changed. The darkness seemed to lose its oppressiveness, and he felt the surrounding presence of One who loved him and was watching over his every step.

You can experience the same sense of security when you realize that behind this universe there is a Father who created you, who loves you, and who has a purpose for you.

Our Creator-Father Is from Everlasting

Continuing with our examination of our Father-Creator, we will see next that God Himself is without beginning or end:

Before the mountains were born or you brought forth the earth and the world, from everlasting to everlasting you are God.
(Psalm 90:2)

Notice that the psalmist did not say, "You *were* God," or, "You *will be* God." He said, "*You **are** God.*" God lives in the eternal present. He has no beginning and no end. He exists forever, and He is the Source of all that has come into being.

The Alpha and the Omega

The eternal God is both beginning and ending. In Revelation, we read these words:

"I am the Alpha and the Omega," says the Lord God, "who is, and who was, and who is to come, the Almighty."
(Revelation 1:8)

Alpha is the first letter of the Greek alphabet; *omega* is the last letter. God says, "I am where it all began, and I am where it is all going to end up. *'I am the Alpha and the Omega.'*" This is the same as saying, using the English alphabet, "I am the A and the Z."

God is. God was. God is to come. The past, present, and future all meet in the eternal being of God. The same thought is repeated at the end of the book of Revelation:

> [Jesus said,] *"I am the Alpha and the Omega, the First and the Last, the Beginning and the End."*   (Revelation 22:13)

You can never get outside of God. He was before you, and He will continue to exist for the rest of time into eternity.

The Author and Perfecter of Our Faith

Not only is God the beginning, but He also takes responsibility for everything He has begun. God never begins something He is not going to see through to the end. He never leaves any of His purposes half-finished. He never has to stop in the middle of His plan and say, "I really don't know what to do with this from here on." Similarly, He never has to say, "I just can't accomplish what I set out to do." Those words are not found in God's vocabulary.

In Hebrews 12:2, we are encouraged to look toward Jesus as *"the author and perfecter [*"finisher"* KJV, NKJV] of our faith."* Our faith begins with Him, and our faith culminates in Him. He has not begun something in our lives that He is unable or unwilling to complete. Just as we trust Him for our beginning, we can trust Him to carry us to completion.

Paul gave the same assurance, which he expressed to the Christians in Philippi:

> *Being confident of this, that he who began a good work in you will carry it on to completion until the day of Christ Jesus.*
> (Philippians 1:6)

God has begun His work in each of us. He will see it through; and when He is finished, it will be perfect. There will be no way to improve upon His work. When you and I understand that

God takes complete responsibility for our lives, we can have confidence. We no longer have to feel like snowflakes—just drifting. Many times, I have told people, "You're not an 'accident waiting to happen.' God has begun a work in your life, and He's going to complete that work. You don't need to be anxious. You just need to trust Him."

> *Just as we trust Jesus for our beginning,*
> *we can trust Him to carry us to completion.*

Our Creator-Father Is Our Salvation

In addition to all that we have seen thus far, this wonderful God Himself—our Creator, our Father—is our salvation. It is most important to understand that salvation is in God Himself. No one less than God could be our salvation. Isaiah testified to this truth:

> *Surely God is my salvation; I will trust and not be afraid. The*
> *LORD, the LORD, is my strength and my song; he has become*
> *my salvation.*   (Isaiah 12:2)

I am sorry for people who try to find salvation in a church, in the law, in a doctrine, or in a denomination. How flimsy and how incapable these substitutes are of providing the salvation we need. In contrast, when we comprehend that our salvation is in God Himself, then we can say, as Isaiah said, "*I will trust and not be afraid.*" Knowing that God is our salvation gives us confidence and security; it removes fear and anxiety.

Our problem today in the Christian church is that we are prone to be extremely self-centered and earth-centered. In reality, there is no peace, no security, and no confidence for those whose lives, thoughts, and purposes are centered entirely on themselves.

There was a period in the history of astronomy when it was believed that the earth was the center of the universe and that the sun, the other stars, and the other planets revolved around the earth. Then, along came an astronomer named Copernicus (and later Kepler and Galileo) who declared that the earth is not the center of the universe; rather, the sun is the center of our solar system. This concept became known as the "Copernican Revolution" because it revolutionized the way human beings thought about the universe.

We need a similar kind of revolution in our thinking today. We are too earth-centered. We need to see that we are not the center of our personal universe. Jesus Christ, the Sun of Righteousness (see Malachi 4:2), is the center. We revolve around Him.

When we are willing to acknowledge this fact, it takes away our sense of insecurity and instability. As long as we are relying on our own efforts and our own abilities, we will never be secure. We will find true security only when we are able to rest in the fact that God is the one and only Source of our salvation.

5

GOD IS IN TOTAL CONTROL

Having recognized that God is behind the created universe, let us go on to examine a related truth: Everything has its source and its fulfillment in God. This truth was summed up simply but profoundly by Paul in his letter to the Romans. Referring to God, he wrote, "For from him and through him and to him are all things" (Romans 11:36).

I am impressed by the fact that in this entire verse, as expressed in the English language, there is not one word that has more than one syllable. There are twelve words of just one syllable—and yet you could not say anything more important or more profound than those words. "For from him and through him and to him are all things." Everything comes from God; everything comes through God; and everything comes to its fulfillment in God.

From this verse, are you able to catch just a glimpse of God's supreme sovereignty over the entire universe? There is nothing in the universe that God does not control—from the largest to the smallest. Let us consider some statements in the Scriptures that make this truth clear.

God Controls the Stars

[God] *determines the number of the stars* [we know there are billions upon billions of them] *and calls them each by name. Great is our Lord and mighty in power; his understanding has no limit.* (Psalm 147:4–5)

There is no limit to God's knowledge and understanding. There is nothing that escapes His attention. The prophet Isaiah said,

> *Lift your eyes and look to the heavens: who created all these [the starry hosts]? He who brings out the starry host one by one, and calls them each by name. Because of his great power and mighty strength, not one of them is missing.*
>
> (Isaiah 40:26)

How that impresses me! God deals with each of the billions upon billions of stars individually, calling them by name. Not only does He know them by name, but He also keeps the stars in place by His power, His knowledge, and His strength. I would like to quote here from one of my earlier books, entitled *Through the Psalms with Derek Prince*. In that work, I made the following comment about Psalm 147:4–5, particularly the phrase "[God] *determines the number of the stars.*" Here is what I wrote:

> The psalmist gives us an objective, scientific standard by which to measure the knowledge and power of the Lord. Human astronomers would not dare to calculate the number of stars in the universe. They do tell us, however, that it amounts to billions upon billions. Yet God knows the exact number of the stars. He is in direct contact with each one and He controls its movements.[1]

So totally accurate and reliable are the movements of the stars that astronomers can compute mathematically where each star was located thousands of years ago and where it will be situated thousands of years from now. But let us never attribute this precision to some mindless, impersonal force or "law." Behind it all is the infinite wisdom of a Creator whose concern extends to the remotest corner of His universe.

---

1. Derek Prince, *Through the Psalms with Derek Prince* (Grand Rapids, MI: Chosen Books [a division of Baker Book House Company], 1983, 2002), 210.

Furthermore, the psalmist tells us *how* God controls the stars: *"He...calls them each by name"* (Psalm 147:4). In the Bible, a name expresses the essential individual character of the person or object named. To God, even the stars are not mere mindless conformations of matter to be identified only by location or magnitude. Each has its own name. And each responds to that name when God calls it.

God Controls the Course of Human History

There was a great Gentile ruler, Nebuchadnezzar, king of Babylon, who had a head-on encounter with the power and wisdom of God. When Nebuchadnezzar declared his own greatness and self-sufficiency, God humbled him so that, for seven years, he was forced to act like a beast. The Scriptures tell us that Nebuchadnezzar went naked in the fields, eating grass, and that his hair and nails grew out like the feathers and talons of birds. Later, after Nebuchadnezzar had learned his lesson, God restored his sanity and his kingdom to him. (See Daniel 4:4–37.) Here is how Nebuchadnezzar summed up the lesson he had learned about the true God, the Lord:

> *For His dominion is an everlasting dominion, and His kingdom is from generation to generation. All the inhabitants of the earth are reputed as nothing; He does according to His will in the army of heaven and among the inhabitants of the earth. No one can restrain His hand or say to Him, "What have You done?"*   (Daniel 4:34–35 NKJV)

In this declaration, Nebuchadnezzar recognized the following truth: God is totally sovereign in the affairs of human beings. All kingdoms, all nations, and all governments are answerable to Him. He disposes of them according to His wisdom. He raises them up, and He puts them down. He enlarges them and then reduces them again. God is in total control.

Human history is not a series of unplanned events that no one understands and no one controls. Behind it all is the same

Person who is behind the whole universe: God, the Creator of the stars and the Creator of man. *"No one can restrain His hand,"* Nebuchadnezzar said, *"or say to Him, 'What have You done?'"* No one can frustrate God's plan.

This same truth is applied to nations in Psalm 33:

> The LORD *foils the plans of the nations; he thwarts the purposes of the peoples. But the plans of the* LORD *stand firm forever, the purposes of his heart through all generations.*
>
> (Psalm 33:10–11)

Ultimately, all history will evidence the outworking of God's eternal purpose. There is no force in human history that can resist or frustrate the plan of God.

God Controls the Destinies of Individuals

God's total control—in the very best sense of the word—applies as well to individuals. In the book of Job, we read how Job was permitted to go through tremendous trials and sufferings. In the end, however, Job had a personal revelation of the living God that was more valuable than all the wealth he had lost. Indeed, that personal revelation made his sufferings seem insignificant in comparison. After receiving the revelation, Job declared to the Lord, *"I know that you can do all things; no plan of yours can be thwarted"* (Job 42:2).

When you and I come to the same place that Job did—where we truly understand that God can do all things and that no plan of His can ever be thwarted—there is really no more room for worry or alarm. The knowledge that God can do all things should give us total peace and security, because we who believe in Christ are a part of His plan. Paul made this clear in his letter to the Ephesians:

> In [Jesus Christ] *we were also chosen, having been predestined according to the plan of* [God] *who works out everything in conformity with the purpose of his will.* (Ephesians 1:11)

Please lay hold of this statement: "[God] *works out everything in conformity with the purpose of his will.*" Nothing is outside His control. Nothing slips through His fingers. He forgets nothing. He overlooks nothing. He is perplexed by nothing. He never has an emergency. Everything is under His control.

Furthermore, if you believe in Jesus Christ, everything in your life is designed to fulfill God's sovereign, eternal plan for you. Paul made this truth abundantly plain:

> *And we know that in all things God works for the good of those who love him, who have been called according to his purpose.* (Romans 8:28)

It does not matter what happens in your life. You may encounter disappointments, frustrations, trials, and dangers. But, behind it all, you can know for certain that God is working everything together for your good.

People often use the above familiar verse in some general sense to mean that everything always turns out all right. However, for that to be fully true, we have to meet three conditions:

1. We must love God—this promise applies only to those who love God.

2. We must be called by God. This means that we must know what God has called us to be and to do.

3. We must be walking in God's purpose for us.

The good news is that if you and I fulfill these three conditions, we know that God causes everything that happens to us to work together for our good.

In summary: God controls the stars. He controls human history. He controls the lives of individuals. Above all, He controls and works out His purposes in the lives of those of us who love Him and who believe in Jesus Christ.

*When we understand that God can do all things
and that none of His plans can be thwarted,
there is no room for worry or alarm.*

God has a good plan for each of us, and He will see it through to the end. No one can frustrate that plan. This is total security in God!

Perhaps you have been struggling in life as a result of not knowing that God is in control. You may not have realized how much the Lord desires to direct the affairs and outcomes of your life. Perhaps you have never acknowledged these truths, but you desire to do so now. In response, would you pray this simple prayer with me now?

Dear Lord, in recognition of the truths I have just read, I want to make the following declarations: You are in control of the universe; You are in control of human history; You are in control of present world events; and, most of all, You are in control of the destiny of each person You have created—including me.

With this prayer, I recognize Your loving care and direction in my life. I renew my commitment to Jesus Christ as my Lord and Savior, and I affirm Your word for me as a believer. I love You, Lord. I believe I am called by You, and I express my intention to walk in Your purposes for me. Because that is true, You are working everything in my life for the good of Your purposes for me.

I take my hands off the reins of my life, and I turn them fully over to You. I thank You, Lord, that You are now in control of every aspect of my life. Amen.

6

SEVEN STAGES IN GOD'S PLAN

In the previous chapter, we were able to see how everything in our lives is working out God's plan for us, as long as we meet His conditions. Just to affirm that truth, let us turn again to Romans 8:28, using a different Bible translation: *"And we know that God causes all things to work together for good to those who love God, to those who are called according to His purpose"* (NASB). In the two verses that follow Romans 8:28, Paul describes how God goes about working His plan into each of our lives. Paul shows us that there are seven successive stages in the outworking of God's purposes:

For those whom He foreknew, He also predestined to become conformed to the image of His Son, so that He would be the firstborn among many brethren; and these whom He predestined, He also called; and these whom He called, He also justified; and these whom He justified, He also glorified.

(Romans 8:29–30 NASB)

These, then, are the seven successive stages in the conception and outworking of God's plan:

1. God foreknew us.
2. God chose us.
3. God predestined us.
4. God called us.
5. God saved us.
6. God justified us.
7. God glorified us.

A Complete Picture

To get a more complete idea of these stages in God's plan and how they relate to one another, we need to combine the above passage from Romans with two other portions of Scripture from the New Testament. When we put all these verses together, we will see the significance of the seven successive stages in God's total plan.

Let's begin to get a fuller picture by looking at a passage from the book of Ephesians:

> *Blessed be the God and Father of our Lord Jesus Christ, who has blessed us with every spiritual blessing in the heavenly places in Christ, just as He chose us in Him before the foundation of the world, that we would be holy and blameless before Him. In love He predestined us to adoption as sons through Jesus Christ to Himself, according to the kind intention of His will.* (Ephesians 1:3–5 NASB)

Here, the same truths we saw earlier are set forth: God has a plan, He is working it out, and we who believe in Jesus are the very center of that plan. Amazing though it may seem, God's eternal design actually revolves around us. In describing the fulfillment of that plan, Paul added a stage that he did not mention in Romans 8. In Ephesians 1:4, we read, "[God] *chose us in Him* [Christ] *before the foundation of the world.*"

God chose us in Christ. It is important for us to realize that this choice did not take place in time, or at some point in human history. God made this choice before the foundation of the world! That is a staggering thought—one that we will unfold more fully a little later. In the list I laid out above, I slotted this truth in second place among the seven stages, because, like the first point, it also occurred in eternity.

Amazing though it may seem,
God's eternal design actually revolves around us.

There is one other point from the Bible that adds to our picture of the seven stages of God's complete plan. In the following passage from 2 Timothy, we see that, as part of His plan, God *saved* us. (In natural sequence, I placed this act of God in fifth position.)

God…has saved us and called us with a holy calling, not according to our works, but according to His own purpose and grace which was granted us in Christ Jesus from all eternity.
(2 Timothy 1:8–9 NASB)

Like the emphasis in the Ephesians verses, Paul underscored to Timothy that God's plan did not begin in time but in eternity. His plan was not an afterthought—an emergency strategy He devised when problems began to develop with humanity. Rather, God's plan was conceived and settled in His mind before He inaugurated history. As we saw above, the *New American Standard Bible* translates this concept as "…*from all eternity*." The *New King James Version* says, "…*before time began*."

We need a different perspective—an eternal perspective—about ourselves and our circumstances. We must look away from our present problems, irritations, and worries. We need to, as Isaiah said, "*lift* [our] *eyes and look to the heavens*…[to] *the starry host*" (Isaiah 40:26). We need to ponder the One who created and controls the universe. We need to see that the God who controls all is the same God who has a plan that He is working out in our lives. We need to see that He is so gracious and so wonderful that, through His precious Word, He reveals to us the way this plan is going to be carried out.

The Seven Stages

If we put together the various passages of Scripture we have just considered, we can understand the seven successive stages of God's plan in their natural order. Let us review these stages in preparation for exploring them in greater detail in coming chapters.

1. God Foreknew Us

First, God foreknew us. He has total knowledge, a fact that we will examine more closely in the next chapter. God bases everything on His knowledge. You may ask, regarding a particular circumstance, "How did God know that it would all work out that way?" God is aware of everything. The past, the present, and the future alike are known to Him. It is extremely important to see that everything proceeds from God's foreknowledge. There is nothing random, impulsive, or casual about the way God works. He acts from full knowledge.

2. God Chose Us

Second, God chose us on the basis of His foreknowledge. He chose us to be His own possession for a special purpose. *"Blessed be the God and Father of our Lord Jesus Christ, who has blessed us with every spiritual blessing in the heavenly places in Christ, just as He chose us in Him before the foundation of the world, that we would be holy and blameless before Him"* (Ephesians 1:3–4 NASB).

3. God Predestined Us

Having chosen us, God predestined us. *Predestined* is a word that some people dislike or find frightening. But, in simple language, here is the meaning of the word in the context of these seven stages of God's plan: "He worked out the course that our lives were to take so that His purposes would be fulfilled."

I trust you can see the simple, logical outworking of God's plan? All these steps must go together, and they must go in this order. God foreknew us. On the basis of His foreknowledge, He chose us. To make His choice effective, He predestined us—He worked out in advance the course our lives were to take. Each of these steps took place in eternity, before creation began. Before history was ever set in motion, God conceived these purposes and worked out how He would implement them.

4. God Called Us

Now we move out of eternity and into time. There is a very important moment in each of our lives—it is the point at which the eternal purpose of God impacts us individually. As God calls us, His purpose comes out of eternity into time and into our lives.

Two of the meanings of the verb *to call* are: "to invite" and "to summon." God's calling is an invitation; but it also carries with it all the authority of a king's summons.

5. God Saved Us

The next stage is that we were invited to join God's family through faith in Jesus Christ. When we responded positively to that call, God saved us, and we entered into salvation. We were saved from sin—from its guilt, from its power, and from its defilement. God has provided a total salvation through Jesus Christ.

6. God Justified Us

When we have been saved, God justifies us. The word *justified* is a somewhat technical theological term. It carries various meanings that all go together: "to acquit," "to reckon righteous," and "to make righteous." Therefore, on the basis of the fact that we were saved through faith in Christ, God acquitted us of all guilt, He reckoned us righteous, and, in the process of time, He makes us righteous. However, justification is not the last stage we experience.

7. God Glorified Us

I believe that the thinking of most Christians stops at the concept of being justified. But God did not stop there. The seventh phase is altogether marvelous: *He glorified us.*

The Bible says we are justified through the resurrection of Christ. But we are glorified through the ascension of Christ. You and I are identified with Christ in each of these aspects: His death, His burial, His resurrection, and His ascension. All these steps lead toward our goal—to share Christ's glory and to take our place with Him on His throne throughout eternity. The destination of our journey is to share God's glory on the throne with Jesus Christ forever.

Let us now consider each successive stage of God's plan in detail.

7

FIRST STAGE: FOREKNOWN

The first stage of God's plan is "He foreknew us." We have seen that, in eternity, God foreknew, chose, and predestined us according to His purpose. His plan always begins with His foreknowledge. The apostle Paul wrote,

> For those whom [God] foreknew, He also predestined to become conformed to the image of His Son.
> (Romans 8:29 NASB)

The apostle Peter expressed the same revelation, but he applied it specifically to God's choice of us:

> Peter, an apostle of Jesus Christ, to those who reside as aliens, scattered throughout Pontus, Galatia, Cappadocia, Asia, and Bithynia, who are chosen according to the foreknowledge of God the Father.... (1 Peter 1:1–2 NASB)

These two Scripture passages affirm that God's foreknowledge always comes first. Out of His foreknowledge proceeds His choice, and out of His choice comes His predestination. *Foreknowledge* simply means that God knows in advance. It is part of His total knowledge. I believe there is no attribute of God more awesome than His knowledge. When we contemplate the characteristics of God, we have to bow in reverence and worship.

God Knows Everything

Let us briefly summarize the extent of what God knows. First of all, very simply, He knows everything! We should never get away from that fact. John wrote, *"God is greater than our hearts, and he knows everything"* (1 John 3:20).

Do you know what *"everything"* means? It means: everything. There is absolutely nothing in the past, the present, or the future—here on earth or in the remotest part of the universe—that God does not know. He knows the biggest things and He knows the smallest things. The following are several matters, large and small, that God fully knows.

God Knows the Stars

Earlier, we saw that God has intimate, personal knowledge of the stars. Psalm 147:4 says, *"He determines the number of the stars and calls them each by name,"* and Isaiah 40:26 affirms, *"He...brings out the starry host one by one, and calls them each by name."* Although there are billions upon billions of stars, God knows each one exactly. He knows the name of each one. He calls each one by name, and they all respond to His call. That is a wonderful thought.

God Knows the Sparrows

Not only does God know the stars, but, coming down a little lower, He also knows the sparrows, which are among the commonest birds in creation. Sparrows can be found in almost all areas of the world. In my travels to many nations, I cannot think of a single country where I have not seen sparrows. These birds are esteemed very little; nobody thinks much about them. If a dead sparrow were found in a gutter somewhere, few people would give it a second thought. But what is God's opinion of sparrows? Jesus said, *"Are not two sparrows sold for a penny? Yet not one of them will fall to the ground apart from the will of your Father"* (Matthew 10:29). The above verse says that two sparrows are sold for one penny, but in another place, Jesus said, *"Are not five sparrows sold for two pennies? Yet not one of them is forgotten by God"* (Luke 12:6).

Notice the mathematics of these two statements. If you could get two sparrows for one penny, then, by the same reckoning, you should get four sparrows for two cents. But, apparently, when you invested two cents, you got five sparrows—the extra sparrow was free. Jesus said that even that fifth sparrow is remembered by God.

I once heard somebody make the following statement, and it brought tears to my eyes: "God takes time to attend a sparrow's funeral." We pay little attention to sparrows; we consider them to be very insignificant. But God knows each one of them, and not one falls to the ground without the Father's knowledge.

God Knows the Number of Hairs on Our Head

Here is another fact God knows that we certainly do not know—the number of hairs on our head! Jesus said, *"Even the very hairs of your head are all numbered"* (Matthew 10:30; see also Luke 12:7). None of us could accurately count the number of hairs on our own head. Some of us have a lot of hair, and others have only a little; but even for those of us who have only a little, we still cannot count all the individual strands of hair. Yet this statement by Jesus attests that God knows the number of hairs on the head of every human being in the world today.

God Knows Us Fully

Moreover, God knows each of us in totality. There is a beautiful passage in Psalm 139 in which King David expressed his wonder at God's knowledge of him. David began with what I would call a gasp of astonishment:

> O LORD, *You have searched me and known me. You know when I sit down and when I rise up; You understand my*

thought from afar. You scrutinize my path and my lying down, and are intimately acquainted with all my ways. Even before there is a word on my tongue, behold, O LORD, You know it all. You have enclosed me behind and before, and laid Your hand upon me. Such knowledge is too wonderful for me; it is too high, I cannot attain to it. Where can I go from Your Spirit? Or where can I flee from Your presence?

(Psalm 139:1–7 NASB)

Think of what David was saying. *God knows our thoughts at a distance.* I once heard a man who had this revelation from God: "Men's thoughts sound as loud in heaven as their voices do on earth." That revelation was a shock to me. But that is what David was indicating here: "*You understand my thought from afar. You scrutinize my path and my lying down.*" In other words, "You know the way I walk; You know where I am to be found at any moment." "*You…are intimately acquainted with all my ways. Even before there is a word on my tongue,…You know it all.*" God knows what we are going to say before we speak it. "*You have enclosed me behind and before*"—"You are all around me." "*You…laid Your hand upon me.*"

Surely, when we consider all these truths, we have to echo the words of David: "*Such knowledge is too wonderful for me; it is too high, I cannot attain to it.*"

Then David said, "*Where can I go from Your Spirit?*" God's Spirit is the key to how God knows everything in the whole universe. The Spirit of God permeates the entire universe. There is no place where the Spirit of God is not present; and, through His Spirit, God knows every item that is on this list we have been examining.

"Men's thoughts sound as loud in heaven
as their voices do on earth."

God Knows Us Personally

Further on in Psalm 139, we see that David spoke about God's personal knowledge of him:

> *For You formed my inward parts; You wove me in my mother's womb.*   (Psalm 139:13 NASB)

David said that before he was born into the world, God was forming him in his mother's womb.

> *I will give thanks to You, for I am fearfully and wonderfully made; wonderful are Your works, and my soul knows it very well. My frame was not hidden from You, when I was made in secret, and skillfully wrought in the depths of the earth.*
> (Psalm 139:14–15 NASB)

Seeing David's response to this fact, I have to confess that I feel the same as he did. When I consider God's knowledge, I am overwhelmed with a sense of praise and awe.

It is amazing to think that God made man out of the dust. (See Genesis 2:7.) But it is even more amazing to realize that He formed that dust in the depths of the earth before He ever used it to make man. God did not just begin with the dust—He began with the chemical processes in the earth that ultimately produced the dust with which He made us.

Continuing his commentary on this amazing process, David said,

> *Your eyes have seen my unformed substance; and in Your book were all written the days that were ordained for me, when as yet there was not one of them.*   (Psalm 139:16 NASB)

David was saying to the Lord, "You've known every process that my body would pass through. You've known when each of my members was to be formed. You've known what day every event would take place in my life. There is nothing that You haven't known—not merely now but in advance."

God's Knowledge Is from Eternity

If we combine David's revelation with the words of Paul and Peter at the beginning of this chapter, we see that God's knowledge is from eternity. Through His Spirit, God knows the past, the present, and the future; the small and the great; the important and the insignificant; what we are like on the inside and what we are like on the outside—our physical nature and our emotional makeup. God foreknows and knows it all. Everything in God's plan for us and for the universe is based upon His foreknowledge. Every aspect of His purposes proceeds from His foreknowledge.

8

SECOND STAGE: CHOSEN

The second stage in God's plan is "He chose us." First He foreknew us, then He chose us. As we pick up our discussion from prior chapters, let us review some Scriptures.

The Responsibility Is God's

First, let's recall these words from Ephesians:

Blessed be the God and Father of our Lord Jesus Christ, who has blessed us with every spiritual blessing in the heavenly places in Christ, just as He chose us in Him before the foundation of the world, that we would be holy and blameless before Him. (Ephesians 1:3–4 NASB)

Everything in those verses centers on the fact that God chose us and that His plan is being worked out in us based upon His choice. According to Paul, God chose us *"that we would be holy and blameless before Him."* I have to say that if God had not chosen us, I would have no faith that the holiness Paul speaks of could ever happen. My faith is based on the fact that God, not I, made the choice. If God made the choice, then, in a certain sense, I can say with reverence, "It's His responsibility to see that it happens."

The Initiative Is God's

For our next point, let's look once again at the following passage from 1 Peter 1:

> *Peter, an apostle of Jesus Christ, to those who reside as aliens, scattered throughout Pontus, Galatia, Cappadocia, Asia, and Bithynia, who are chosen according to the foreknowledge of God the Father....* (1 Peter 1:1–2 NASB)

As I pointed out, God foreknows, and then He chooses—and His choice is always based on His knowledge. These facts should relieve us of a lot of anxiety! If God has chosen us to do something, He has done so because He knows it is by His grace that we will be able to complete the task for which He chose us. It is very important to understand that, in all God's dealings with humanity—as a matter of fact, with the whole universe—He always retains the initiative. In fact, the initiative never passes out of His hands.

I want to illustrate this truth from various aspects of God's activity recorded in the New Testament. It is important to dwell on this reality because, today, many Christians scarcely ever leave the initiative with God. Instead, we are inclined to think that everything depends on what *we* do—even to the point of thinking that if we do not do something, nothing will happen. In a certain sense, that is true. However, it is not the total, or real, truth.

The real truth is that God set everything into being. For instance, in the new birth, or salvation, the initiative is with God. Many people think they were born again because *they* decided it. However, that is not really the truth. *We are born again because God decided it.* We have to *respond* to God's decision, but without His decision, it never could have happened by us alone.

> *In the exercise of His will [God] brought us forth by the word of truth, so that we would be a kind of first fruits among His creatures.* (James 1:18 NASB)

Notice the first part of the verse: *"In the exercise of His will [God] brought us forth by the word of truth."* We were born again because God chose to make it so. The *New International Version* translates this portion of the verse, *"He **chose** to give us birth through the word of truth."* Always remember that the new birth proceeds not from our choice but from God's choice.

This is also true of salvation, which is an aspect of the experience of being chosen. Paul wrote to the Christians in Thessalonica:

> But we should always give thanks to God for you, brethren beloved by the Lord, because God has chosen you from the beginning for salvation through sanctification by the Spirit and faith in the truth.　　　(2 Thessalonians 2:13 NASB)

God chose you for salvation. You were not saved because you chose it. You were saved because God chose it. Never pull the initiative out of God's hands. As long as you see that the initiative is in God's hands, you can rest—you can feel confident and secure. However, if you think that everything starts with you, you will never have real inner peace and rest. You will always be uneasy.

If God has chosen us to do something,
it is because He knows that, by His grace,
we will be able to complete the task.

God Called, or "Appointed," Us

The same principle—that the initiative rests with God—is true of our calling. Jesus said to His apostles,

> You did not choose Me but I chose you, and appointed you that you would go and bear fruit, and that your fruit would

remain, so that whatever you ask of the Father in My name
He may give to you.   (John 15:16 NASB)

Jesus was saying, "You didn't choose Me in order to become apostles. I chose you." This is true of every function in the body of Christ. We do not choose our calling; we have a calling because the Lord has chosen it for us. Peter applied this truth to his own experience. Speaking to the council gathered in Jerusalem, he said,

Brethren, you know that in the early days God made a choice
among you, that by my mouth the Gentiles would hear the
word of the gospel and believe.   (Acts 15:7 NASB)

Peter went to the household of Cornelius, a Roman centurion and a Gentile—not because he chose to, but because God chose him to go. (See Acts 10.) Everything significant in the body of Christ and in the service of the Lord proceeds out of God's choice, not out of man's choice.

The principle of God's initiative may be seen as well in the life of the apostle Paul. He had a marvelous revelation of Jesus on the Damascus road, after which he went into Damascus and remained for three days without being able to see. When Paul had spent three days in blindness, taking neither food nor drink, God sent another disciple, Ananias, to pray for Paul so that he might receive his sight and be filled with the Holy Spirit. When Ananias encountered Paul, he said to him,

The God of our fathers has chosen you that you should know
His will, and see the Just One [Jesus], and hear the voice of
His mouth. For you will be His witness to all men of what you
have seen and heard.   (Acts 22:14–15 NKJV)

Paul did not become an apostle because he chose that calling for himself. In fact, had the decision been left to Paul, he never would have chosen it. Left to himself, becoming an apostle would have been the furthest idea from his thinking. Additionally, no one in the early church would ever have chosen Paul to be an apostle. He would have been at the bottom of the list. But God made the choice. *"The God of our fathers,"* Ananias said, *"has chosen you that you should know His will, and see the Just One, and hear the voice of His mouth. For you will be His witness to all men…."*

Confidence in God's Choice

When God makes the choice, such as He did in the above examples from the New Testament, a certain confidence is released. Ananias did not say to Paul, "God wants you to be His witness," but rather, *"You **will be** His witness."* Why would Paul be God's witness? Because God had chosen him. If we would have that attitude in our lives, it would release tremendous confidence in us. If we would find out what God has chosen us to be, instead of trying to be something on our own, then we would have a quiet confidence in our hearts and minds. We would know that the Lord will empower us to be whatever He has chosen us to be.

Again, we need to emphasize that God's choice is based on His foreknowledge. And *foreknowledge* simply means "knowing in advance." The life of Abraham is a very clear example of God's foreknowledge. The Lord said the following about Abraham:

> *Shall I hide from Abraham what I am doing, since Abraham shall surely become a great and mighty nation, and all the nations of the earth shall be blessed in him? For **I have known him**, in order that he may command his children and his household after him, that they may keep the way of the LORD, to do righteousness and justice, that the LORD may bring to Abraham what He has spoken to him.*
>
> (Genesis 18:17–19 NKJV)

God chose Abraham because He had known him. He knew Abraham was a man in whom He could fulfill His will—a man who would do all He wanted him to accomplish.

It is so comforting and so important to understand that God's choice in our lives is based upon His knowledge of us. Please, never allow yourself to hold an attitude that says, "Well, God has chosen me to do something, but I can't do it." God knows you can accomplish His will. If He didn't believe you could do it, He wouldn't have chosen you. He chose you on the basis of His knowledge of you.

It is very interesting that the *New American Standard Bible* translates Genesis 18:19 not as *"I have known him"* but *"I have chosen him."* Those are two ways of translating the same Hebrew word. Without going into all the reasons why it could be translated either way, the main point it brings out is that God's knowledge leads to His choice.

Let God Choose

You and I need to apply the reality of God's choice to our own lives. Here is a beginning piece of advice: Never try to be something God has not chosen you to be. Do not make your own plan—and do not depend upon the best you can do—because that is not sufficient. *Find out what God has chosen you to be.* It may be very different from what you have anticipated or planned for yourself. But when you discover what God's choice is, then you can know for certain that it is based upon His knowledge of you. He knows you well enough for you to be confident that, by His grace, you can be and do all He has chosen you to be and to do.

To me, my daughter Jessika is a beautiful picture of God's choice. For many years, my first wife, Lydia, and I were responsible for a college that trained African teachers in Kenya. We were very busy, and Lydia was well up in years, being somewhat older than I.

One evening, at about half-past six, a strange group appeared on our doorstep: a white lady and a black African couple. The white lady was carrying a little black baby girl wrapped in a dirty towel. We asked, "Why have you come?"

They said, "This little girl's mother died when she was born. A social worker found her on the floor of the hut and took her to the local hospital. They've looked after her for six months, but they have now said, 'This is a hospital and not a children's home. We can't keep her any longer.' We have been going around this part of Kenya for three days looking for a family—Asian, African, or European—that would take this little baby. We heard that you took in children."

My wife replied to them, "That was years ago. We're much too old to do that now. Besides, we're so busy with our educational work, and we really don't have any time for a little baby—and a sick baby at that."

So, this group of people said, "We're so tired. Would you let us just sit down for half an hour and rest?" We invited them in, and at the end of the half hour, they got up to go. When they did, the white lady carrying the little baby passed by me. As she went past, the baby stretched out one hand toward me, as if to say, "What are you going to do about me?" I am not a fanciful person, but the baby's action was so unusual as to be arresting to me.

At that moment, I looked at my wife. Normally, we would never make a decision like that without talking to each other privately. But I said, "Maybe we'll change our minds." Lydia—God bless her—said, "Give me a week to get some baby clothes and a crib, and then bring her back."

That is how we got our ninth daughter, who today is a sweet Christian woman serving the Lord. There were millions of African baby girls, and God laid His hand on this one—she was God's sovereign choice for us. As we will see in the next chapter, God's choice is due to His predestination. Jessika was predestined by God to become our daughter. I have always been glad that God made that choice and that we responded with the decision to take her.

Let me close by making what could be a rather controversial statement. Why is it controversial? Because I believe it is the opposite of much of the thinking in the contemporary church. Here it is: *God makes His selection. He does not call for volunteers.* A lot of people in the church have the idea that they can volunteer for something, and God will accept that. That is not true. God makes His choice, and He does not ask us to volunteer. He simply asks us to respond to His choice.

Never try to be something God has not chosen you to be.

It may be that you have never actively responded to God's calling upon you. This would be an ideal moment to do so. If you would like to respond to God's call on your life, please make this declaration in simple faith:

> Lord, I thank You that, by Your initiative and foreknowledge, You have called me. I respond positively right now to Your call upon my life. It is not I who have chosen You—it is You who have chosen me. You have a purpose and a plan for my life. I am not an "accident waiting to happen"— I am Your servant, chosen by You and called to do Your will. I acknowledge and gratefully accept the fact that You have chosen me and that You have called me. Thank You, dear Lord. Amen.

Now that you have taken this very important step of acknowledging God's call upon your life, we will move ahead in our teaching to stage three of God's plan for us in eternity.

9

THIRD STAGE: PREDESTINED

The third stage of God's plan for us—which also takes place in eternity—is "He predestined us." The noun *predestination* was formed from the verb *predestined*. As I said earlier, *predestined* is a rather frightening word to many people because they relegate it to some tremendous theological issue about salvation. Consequently, they tend to shy away from it. Actually, its meaning is rather simple: being "predestined" simply means that *God has arranged in advance the course your life is to follow.* The New Testament lays great emphasis on the fact that God has predestined us. In this chapter, we will explore four examples of this truth.

Scriptural Teachings on Predestination

Our first two examples of the fact that God has predestined us are found in Romans 8, where Paul wrote,

> For those whom [God] *foreknew*, **He also predestined** to become conformed to the image of his Son...; and these whom **He predestined**, He also called; and these whom He called, He also justified; and these whom He justified, He also glorified. (Romans 8:29–30 NASB)

In this passage, Paul twice stated that God predestined those whom He called. Please notice *to what* we are predestined, because that is very important. Many people tend to talk about being predestined to heaven or to hell, an approach that often confuses or offends those who listen to them. But Paul said we are predestined *"to become conformed to the image of* [God's] *Son,"* Jesus Christ.

If somebody tells me he is predestined to heaven, yet I see no fruit is his life and no trace of godliness, I might well question the validity of what he is saying. However, if I see somebody who is becoming truly conformed in his life and character to the person and nature of Jesus Christ, then I must conclude that there is only one explanation for it—he must have been predestined. It could not have come about in any other way.

Many people talk about being predestined to heaven or to hell. But Paul said we are predestined "to become conformed to the image of [God's] *Son."*

Then, in Ephesians, Paul provided the third example of the fact that God has predestined us:

> *Blessed be the God and Father of our Lord Jesus Christ, who has blessed us with every spiritual blessing in the heavenly places in Christ, just as He chose us in Him before the foundation of the world, that we would be holy and blameless before Him. In love **He predestined us** to adoption as sons through Jesus Christ to Himself, according to the kind intention of His will, to the praise of the glory of His grace, which He freely bestowed on us in the Beloved* [Jesus].
>
> (Ephesians 1:3–6 NASB)

Not only did God predestine us to be conformed to the image of Christ, but He also predestined us to be adopted to Himself as His children through Jesus Christ. This was His *"kind intention,"* which He settled in eternity. For what purpose are we so predestined? Paul added that all of this is designed to work out *"to the praise of the glory of His grace."*

So, in the above passage, Paul stated three characteristics of our predestination. First, we are predestined to be sons of God by being adopted into His family. Second, our predestination is intended to bring glory to God. And, third, it all happens by His grace.

The ultimate purpose of everything in the universe is to glorify God. In that regard, then, the essence of sin is the failure to glorify God. Paul wrote, *"All have sinned..."* (Romans 3:23). How have all sinned? By *"[falling] short of the glory of God"* (Romans 3:23). Therefore, God's purpose in predestination is to retrieve His glory, which our sin had robbed Him of. He accomplishes all this through His grace—not through our works. He brings us into His family in such a way that our lives bring glory to Him. You and I are realistic enough about ourselves to acknowledge that if something positive does not happen in our lives by God's grace, it is never going to happen.

In this matter of scriptural insights about predestination, I want to add one more quote from Paul, which is our fourth example of this principle:

> *In Him also we have obtained an inheritance, **having been predestined according to His purpose** who works all things after the counsel of His will, to the end that we who were the first to hope in Christ would be to the praise of His glory.*
> (Ephesians 1:10–12 NASB)

Notice again that we are predestined according to the purpose of God, who works all things according to His will. This simple fact should set our hearts at rest. If God has decided to do something, He is going to get it done. And everything He does is for the praise of His glory, which is always His ultimate purpose.

Let me sum up the essence of all these Scriptures in a very simple, practical application that will encourage you greatly: You are not an accident waiting to happen. You are part of an eternal plan. You are destined to become a member of God's family. It is all going to take place through His grace and for His glory. This, in its totality, is complete security.

A Lesson from Jonah

In regard to the practical side of being predestined, we see that God's predestination also provides for our mistakes. We can thank the Lord for that. God anticipates our mistakes and has prepared various ways to deliver us from them by His grace. The life of the prophet Jonah provides a clear picture of this truth.

God called Jonah from the mountains of Galilee to go east to Nineveh. He was to warn that city of impending destruction due to the people's sin. However, Jonah was an Israelite, and Nineveh was the capital of Israel's enemy, Assyria. Jonah did not want to see God spare Nineveh. So, instead of going eastward to Nineveh, he refused his call and went westward.

If you study Jonah's pathway after that refusal of God's call, every step he took was a step down. He went down from the mountains to the foothills, from the foothills to the plain, from the plain to the port, from the port to the harbor, from the harbor to the ship, and from the ship into the sea.

Jonah's downward path should be a warning to each and every one of us not to refuse the call of God on our lives. However, God had His plan worked out: "*The Lord hurled a great wind on the sea and there was a great storm on the sea so that the ship was about to break up*" (Jonah 1:4 NASB). God blocked Jonah's path by a storm, and the sailors ultimately threw Jonah overboard. But later on in that chapter, it says, "*And the Lord appointed a great fish to swallow*

Jonah, and Jonah was in the stomach of the fish three days and three nights" (Jonah 1:17 NASB).

God had prepared the fish. Think about it: If that fish had needed to swim fifty miles to get to Jonah, Jonah would have been dead by the time the fish got there. However, the fish was there waiting for Jonah because God had already provided it. That is God's predestination!

After being three days and three nights in the belly of the fish, Jonah changed his mind. He went back to Nineveh and preached what God had told him to preach—and the city repented. However, Jonah got very angry because he really did not want to see his enemies spared. What was his response? He went off by himself to pout—and he sat down in an exposed area that overlooked the city of Nineveh. It was boiling hot, what they call in Israel a *sirocco*—a terrible hot wind that makes everyone miserable. To protect Jonah from the sun, *"the LORD God appointed a plant and it grew up over Jonah to be a shade over his head to deliver him from his discomfort. And Jonah was extremely happy about the plant"* (Jonah 4:6 NASB).

Well, Jonah was very happy with the plant. But he still was not glad that God had spared Nineveh. Therefore, to teach Jonah a lesson, God caused the plant to wither. *"God appointed a worm when dawn came the next day and it attacked the plant and it withered"* (Jonah 4:7 NASB).

I want you to notice the word *"appointed"* in that verse, as well as in Jonah 1:17. God had appointed a storm, He had appointed a fish, He had appointed a plant, and He had appointed a worm to eat the plant. All these events were prearranged. God knew what Jonah was going to do the first time He called him. God did not approve of what Jonah did. But because Jonah was predestined, ultimately, God got His way.

That should be a word of encouragement to us. Not that we should be disobedient, but that we should know that even if we make mistakes or take a wrong course, God's predestination has taken it into account in advance. He will have the storm, the fish, the plant, the worm, or whatever else is needed to cause us to realign with His way. This brings us back to the original purpose for predestination. What is that purpose? That we might fulfill God's plan for our lives—even in spite of ourselves—in a way that ultimately brings glory to Him.

You are part of an eternal plan. It is all going to take place through God's grace and for His glory.

10

FOURTH STAGE: CALLED

The first three phases of God's plan for us—"He foreknew us," "He chose us," and "He predestined us"—belong to the realm of eternity. They all were complete before time began. I believe it is important to understand this, because it gives us such a different sense of who we are, where we came from, and where we are going. We are not just creatures of time. Our roots are in eternity—in the eternal mind, heart, and counsel of God.

From Eternity into Time

The fourth phase—"He called us"—is different from the first three. At this point, God's plan emerged out of eternity into time. When that happened to each one of us, God made His first impact in our individual lives. That is why the moment when God calls you or me is perhaps the most critical moment of our lives. Our future is decided by our response to His call.

I can remember very vividly my moment of being called by God. It was July 1941, and I was without any background in spiritual understanding or knowledge of the Bible—someone who had completely dropped out of church attendance. I was what you might call a nominal Christian. In that condition, I was suddenly, unexpectedly, and dramatically confronted by God's call. In all my ignorance and all my darkness, I saw one truth by revelation: *I could never expect or claim that God would call to me a second time after that.* I understood what a critical moment this was in my whole life. I had to decide how I was going to respond to God's call. With all my heart, I thank God that, by His grace, I made the right response.

Please note very carefully what I am about to say. If, as you read this, you have a sense that God is calling you—if what I have written here answers to something that is happening right now in your life—I want to tell you very urgently, *this is the most critical moment of your life.* Please give careful heed—not just to me, but to the voice of God as He speaks to you.

Invited and Summoned

The word *call* is somewhat of an Old English word, at least the way it is used in the Bible. As I mentioned earlier, it has two meanings that go together: "to invite" and "to summon." When you receive an invitation, it means you are being asked to participate in something nice. But when you receive a summons, it always represents a mandate from an authority. The call of God is both. It is an invitation to all the blessings of God in Jesus Christ. But it is also a summons from the Ruler of the universe. When we receive God's call, we cannot just shrug our shoulders and say, "Well, I don't feel like accepting." Rather, we must soberly recognize that we are dealing with almighty God.

In all that pertains to this matter of calling, God still retains the initiative. He calls; we answer. However, it is important for us to recognize at this critical point that His call requires a response from us. Again, His foreknowledge, His choice, and His predestination were events that took place in eternity apart from our involvement. But when we are confronted by His call, it is mandatory that we make a response. And I want to repeat: Our response to His call determines all that will follow in our lives.

God's call requires a response from us.

Salvation Is a Call

The proclamation of the gospel is God's invitation, and acceptance of it brings salvation. As Paul explained:

> But we should always give thanks to God for you, brethren beloved by the Lord, because God has chosen you from the beginning for salvation through sanctification by the Spirit and faith in the truth. It was for this He called you through our gospel, that you may gain the glory of our Lord Jesus Christ.
> (2 Thessalonians 2:13–14 NASB)

Paul again emphasized the fact that God chose us; in this case, he wrote about God choosing us for salvation. Paul said that God called us into salvation by the proclamation of the gospel. When the preaching of the gospel comes to us, it is God's call. It is His invitation and/or summons into salvation. Paul concluded the above passage with the following words: "*That you may gain the glory of our Lord Jesus Christ.*" Please remember that everything God does in all His predestination is for the purpose of His glory.

God's choice is expressed in our lives by His calling. Until God calls us, we do not know He has chosen us. But from the moment He calls us onward, we are confronted by the solemn fact that God has chosen us.

We are called into salvation. The acceptance of that calling brings salvation. When we experience salvation, we discover (or should discover) that salvation opens the door into the fulfillment of that for which God called us. This point is very important. Many people who are saved do not realize that when they are *saved*, they are also *called*.

Three Important Aspects of Our Calling

You may not yet feel that you have discovered your calling. Even so, you are called by God. Paul wrote to Timothy,

> [God] *has saved us and called us with a holy calling, not according to our works, but according to His own purpose and grace which was granted us in Christ Jesus from all eternity.*
>
> (2 Timothy 1:9 NASB)

We need to understand the following three aspects of our calling.

1. It Is a Holy Calling

First, our calling is a holy calling. It is something to which we should give our complete attention, and it should take total priority in every aspect of our lives. It is holy and sacred, and we need to treat it as such. You should never let anything come between you and the purpose and call of God in your life.

2. It Is a Calling by Grace

Second, Paul said our calling is not according to our works but *"according to [God's] own purpose and grace."* In other words, our calling and our ability to fulfill it do not depend on our natural ability. It is essential to grasp this truth.

You might say, "How could God call me to do this or that? I don't have the ability." It does not depend on your ability; it depends on His grace. In fact, God's grace begins where your ability ends. As long as you can handle something by yourself, you don't need God's grace.

Never refuse God's calling because you feel unable. Almost every person in the Bible whom God called felt unable. It is probably a good sign if you feel unable. I question whether a person is really called by God if he says, "Well, of course, I can do exactly what

God tells me to do." The first realization that comes to you when you are called is the recognition of your own inability. That realization simply causes you to cast yourself upon the grace and mercy of God.

Let me give you a personal example. I am an only child. I never had brothers or sisters. I was educated in two boarding schools where there were no girls. Then I went to Cambridge University, where girls were very much in the background. At the beginning of World War II, I was called up into the predominantly male British Army, and, in the purpose of God by divine predestination, the army put me in the land of Palestine and ultimately in the city of Jerusalem.

Just before I left the army, I married a Danish lady, Lydia Christensen, a missionary who directed a children's home. At the time, there were eight girls in her home: six Jewish, one Arab, and one English. From the background and experience I just described, you could not have thought of anybody less suitable than I to become the father of eight adopted girls. If people had made a list of possible candidates, my name would not have been on it.

However, God did not consult other people; He did not even consult me! It was divine choice, divine wisdom. The whole experience did me a lot of good. I had to learn that there were other people in the world besides Derek Prince. The point is this: God gave me the grace to do something for which, in the natural, I was completely ill-suited.

---

*God's call should take total priority
in every aspect of our lives.*

---

3. It Is a Calling from Eternity

The third aspect of God's calling is that we are called to fulfill a purpose that was conceived before time began. This truth is exciting to me. I see so many people today just adrift in the sea of time. They have no anchor—they have no past, and they have no future. They are like corks bobbing up and down on the waves. Why? Because they have never apprehended this vision of an eternal God who had a plan for them before time began—and who, in due course, would confront them with His plan when He called them.

The apostle Peter described the appropriate response to God's call: *"Therefore, my brothers, be all the more eager to make your calling and election sure"* (2 Peter 1:10). When you are called, God has done His part. You must now respond. Peter said we should respond by being eager to make our calling and election sure. I would sum up this response in one word: *single-mindedness.* You have to have a single focus. You have to have one goal. You must say, like Paul, *"'This one thing I do,…I press toward the mark for the prize of the high calling of God in Christ Jesus.'* I am not going to be diverted." (See Philippians 3:13–14 KJV.)

Why not take a moment now to say those words to the Lord in regard to your own calling? Please repeat Paul's affirmation out loud as your response to God's call on your life:

Lord, regarding Your call, I echo what Paul said: *"This one thing I do,…I press toward the mark for the prize of the high calling of God in Christ Jesus."* I will not allow myself to be diverted from my calling in God. Amen.

11

FIFTH STAGE: SAVED

As we come to the fifth stage in God's plan for us—"He saved us"—we need to consider what it means to enter into salvation in response to God's call. We must first understand the simple requirements for salvation given in the New Testament. Paul stated them in Romans:

> If you confess with your mouth Jesus as Lord, and believe in your heart that God raised Him from the dead, you will be saved. (Romans 10:9 NASB)

According to that verse, you need to complete just two actions. First, with your heart, you need to believe the record of the New Testament that God raised Jesus from the dead. However, that, in itself, is not enough. To give your assent to what God says, you must actively submit your life to the lordship of Jesus. That means you must personally confess Jesus as Lord. These two simple requirements together—believing in the heart and confessing with the mouth—bring you into salvation.

The Process of Salvation

Salvation brings to us at least four benefits. There were four negative conditions from which we were saved, all of which are related to sin. We were saved from sin in general, but we were specifically saved from its guilt, its condemnation, its power, and its defilement.

Salvation is a process that takes place within us, as described in the following verse:

> [God] *saved us, not on the basis of deeds which we have done in righteousness, but according to His mercy, by the washing of regeneration and renewing by the Holy Spirit.*
>
> (Titus 3:5 NASB)

The process of salvation embraces three activities: *"washing," "regeneration,"* and *"renewing."*

1. Washing

First comes *"washing,"* or cleansing, from the defilement of sin. We are inwardly dirty, and we need to be cleansed. There is only one element that can purify the sinner—the blood of the Lord Jesus Christ. In 1 John 1:7, the apostle John declared that it is the blood of Jesus, God's Son, that purifies us from our sin.

John told us how we can receive this cleansing: *"If we confess our sins, [God] is faithful and righteous to forgive us our sins and to cleanse us from all unrighteousness"* (1 John 1:9 NASB). Please notice that God does not merely forgive our past. That fact, in itself, is wonderful. But He also cleanses us from all the defilement of sin.

2. Regeneration

The second phase of the salvation process is *"regeneration,"* or rebirth. Jesus spoke these very familiar words to Nicodemus: *"Truly, truly, I say to you, unless one is born again he cannot see the kingdom of God"* (John 3:3 NASB).

An alternate translation for *"born again"* is "born from above." Regeneration is a birth that comes from God's realm above. Jesus also said, *"That which is born of the flesh is flesh, and that which is born of the Spirit is spirit"* (John 3:6 NASB). When you were born of your mother, it was a birth that involved your physical body and your fleshly nature. However, that is not the birth that brings you into salvation. Salvation comes through a birth of the Spirit—the Holy Spirit. By that birth, we receive a totally new life that is born into us by the Spirit of God from above. This is the meaning of regeneration, or rebirth.

3. Renewing

The final phrase of the salvation process is *"renewing."* In Christ, we become a *"new creation."* Paul wrote, *"Therefore, if anyone is in Christ, he is a new creation; the old has gone, the new has come!"* (2 Corinthians 5:17). The word *"creation"* is important because the only One who creates is God. Humans can manufacture, repair, or refine, but we cannot create. Yet a new creation is what we need. Our heart and inner being have been so defiled and distorted by the effects of sin that simply repairing them or patching them up would be ineffective. Only a new creation is adequate for God's purpose.

After King David had not only fallen into adultery but also committed a murder to cover it up, he was confronted by the prophet Nathan about the awful condition of his own heart. In Psalm 51:10, he cried out to God in agony, *"Create in me a clean heart, O God"* (nasb). He knew that a truly clean heart must come from God, the Creator; no human process could bring that about.

In these three aspects of the salvation process—cleansing, rebirth, and a new creation—God does something that human beings absolutely cannot do. All this is God's mercy, not His justice. He applies salvation, not according to the deeds of righteousness that we have done, but according to His sovereign mercy.

Only a new creation is adequate for God's purpose.

Salvation Brings Decisive Transitions

This salvation we are speaking of brings about decisive transitions in a person's life. The first is a transition "*from death to life*":

> [Jesus said,] "*I tell you the truth, whoever hears my word and believes him who sent me has eternal life and will not be condemned; he has crossed over from death to life.*"   (John 5:24)

Salvation is the crossing over from death into eternal life.

Second, salvation is a transition *from darkness to light.* Paul wrote, "*For you were once darkness, but now you are light in the Lord*" (Ephesians 5:8).

Third, salvation is a transition *from being a child of wrath to being a child of God.* Paul said, "*Among them* ["*the sons of disobedience*"] *we too* [including himself]...*were by nature children of wrath*" (Ephesians 2:3 NASB; see also verse 2 NASB). And yet, John spoke the following wonderful truths about those children of wrath who receive Jesus: "*To all who received him, to those who believed in his name, he gave the right to become children of God*" (John 1:12–13). It is the decisive act of receiving Jesus that causes a person to be changed from a child of wrath to a child of God. This transition does not come about by joining a church, "turning over a new leaf," or making good resolutions. It happens by receiving Jesus.

A Vital Decision

In regard to salvation, then, we are left with two categories of persons. When we speak of material wealth, we often refer to "the have's" and "the have not's." This concept also applies in the spiritual realm. John summed up the situation as follows:

> And the testimony is this, that God has given us eternal life, and this life is in His Son. He who has the Son has the life; he

who does not have the Son of God does not have the life.

(1 John 5:11–12 NASB)

The question you must answer is, "Do *you* have Jesus?" In Jesus, you have eternal life. If you do not have Jesus—if you have not received Him—you do not have *"the life."* Are you a "have," or are you a "have not"? That is a vital decision every person must make—a critical issue you have to resolve for yourself.

As we end this chapter on salvation, my question to you is this: Why wait? If you have any doubt about your standing with God and would like to resolve this issue once and for all, please take care of the matter now. If you would like to take this vital step, or even if you would like to affirm it again to make the matter sure forever, please pray this prayer with me now:

Dear Jesus, I need this process of salvation to be complete in my life. I desperately need to be cleansed from my sinfulness. I need to be reborn by the Holy Spirit, and I need to be renewed as a new creation in You. I want to move from death to life, from darkness to light, from being a child of wrath to being a child of God. Therefore, I now receive You, Lord Jesus Christ, into my life. I believe in my heart that God raised You from the dead, and I confess with my mouth that You are my Lord. Thank You for Your wonderful salvation. Amen.

12

SIXTH STAGE: JUSTIFIED

As we have learned so far in our discussions about salvation, the essence of receiving salvation is to meet two simple requirements: believing in your heart that God raised Jesus from the dead and confessing with your mouth Jesus as Lord. When you meet those conditions, as you did at the end of the last chapter, you can say, on the basis of the Bible, "I am saved."

Unfortunately, the thinking and the experience of many Christians stops there. However, salvation leads us to the sixth stage: "He justified us." As with the word *predestination*, some people consider *justification* to be a frightening theological word from which they back away. Yet to do so is a great pity, because justification is one of the most glorious truths of the entire Bible.

What Is "Justification"?

What does it mean to be justified? To answer that question, we will look at a succession of definitions. First, to be justified means "to be acquitted of a crime." Justification is heaven's "Not guilty" verdict on your life.

To be justified also means "to be reckoned righteous." When you are justified, God imputes, or imparts, His own righteousness to you.

Finally, to be justified means "to be made righteous." Please do not stop at being "reckoned" righteous—you must be *made* righteous.

Here is my simple explanation of what it means to be justified: "Just-as-if-I'd never sinned." I have been made righteous with the righteousness of God—a righteousness that has never known sin, that has no shadow of guilt, and that has no past to be forgiven. To be made righteous with God's righteousness is the full meaning of justification.

To be justified means "Just-as-if-I'd never sinned."

How Can We Be Righteous?

Justification is the answer to a question Job asked in what is perhaps the oldest book of the Bible. At a time when Job was in tremendous distress, he cried out, *"How can a mortal be righteous before God?"* (Job 9:2). This question is very deep, very profound. Job's friends, who really were not much help to him, all seemed to agree that no one can be righteous before God. To them, it was ridiculous even to talk that way. Thankfully, Job held on to his question. Even though he did not have the answer, he would not abandon the question.

If you want to find the answer to Job's question, a good place to turn is Paul's epistle to the Romans. There, Paul gave the complete answer to the problem expressed by this question: *"How can a mortal be righteous before God?"*

> *But now apart from the Law the righteousness of God has been manifested, being witnessed by the Law and the Prophets, even the righteousness of God through faith in Jesus Christ for all those who believe; for there is no distinction; for all have sinned and fall short of the glory of God, being justified as a gift by His grace through the redemption which is in Christ Jesus.* (Romans 3:21–24 NASB)

Please notice that we are *"justified"*—reckoned righteous—
"as a gift." We cannot earn it, because it is received through God's
grace—not our efforts. This justification occurs through the
redemption that has been provided by the sacrificial death of Jesus
Christ on our behalf.

A Gift by Faith

Paul wrote, *"Therefore, having been justified by faith, we have
peace with God through our Lord Jesus Christ"* (Romans 5:1 NASB).
We receive justification from God as a gift by faith—never by
works, only by believing. If you try to earn it, you will never get
it. You must believe. The problem with many religious people is
that they are trying to earn God's righteousness, something that
cannot be earned.

We see this truth even more clearly further on in the fifth
chapter of Romans, where Paul compared the results of the sin of
Adam with the righteousness of Christ:

> *For if by the transgression of the one, death reigned through
> the one, much more those who receive the abundance of grace
> and of the gift of righteousness will reign in life through the
> One, Jesus Christ.*   (Romans 5:17 NASB)

Paul spoke about receiving *"the abundance of grace and of the gift
of righteousness."* Again, we see by his words that righteousness is
offered to us by God as a gift. When you are saved, God offers you
righteousness as a gift. The basis for this is the exchange that took
place when Jesus died on the cross. Jesus took the place of the sinner,
the unrighteous, and the ungodly. He bore the sinner's condemnation, and He suffered the sinner's punishment. But the other side
of that act is the exchange God offers to us. In 2 Corinthians, Paul
succinctly stated the nature of this exchange. Speaking about Jesus,

he wrote, *"God made him who had no sin to be sin for us, so that in him we might become the righteousness of God"* (2 Corinthians 5:21).

In the exchange on the cross, Jesus was made sin with our sinfulness. He died because *"the wages of sin is death"* (Romans 6:23). But on the other side of that wonderful exchange, we become, in Christ, the righteousness of God.

Please ponder for a moment this phrase from 2 Corinthians 5:21: *"...in him we might become the righteousness of God."* If you are feeling insecure, troubled, or guilty, grasp this truth by faith: You, through faith in Jesus, have been made the righteousness of God. Now take one more moment to consider carefully what the righteousness of God is—a righteousness that has never sinned, has no guilt, and has no dark shadows from the past. Satan can tear your own righteousness to pieces with his accusations. But there is nothing he can say against the righteousness of God. Through the exchange on the cross, God's righteousness is now yours.

If you are feeling troubled or guilty, grasp the truth that, through faith in Jesus, you have been made the righteousness of God.

A Robe of Righteousness

In the Old Testament, the prophet Isaiah gave us a beautiful picture of salvation plus justification. Let me emphasize again that you must not stop at receiving salvation. You must go on to receive justification. Here is a prophetic picture of what salvation will do for God's people:

> *I will rejoice greatly in the LORD, my soul will exult in my God; for He has clothed me with garments of salvation, He*

has wrapped me with a robe of righteousness.

(Isaiah 61:10 NASB)

In this verse, we find Isaiah expressing real excitement. I question whether a person who never gets excited about salvation has much in the way of salvation. I find that the people in the Bible who knew what salvation was got really excited about it. Isaiah said, "*I will rejoice greatly in the LORD, my soul will exult in my God.*"

When God has given you the garments of salvation, please do not refuse the robe of righteousness. Salvation is the first stage; righteousness is the second stage. Why shouldn't you have it? It is God's righteousness. You cannot earn it; it is a gift.

Again, Isaiah used a most beautiful picture when he said, "[God] *has wrapped me with a robe of righteousness.*" Like Isaiah, we can say, "God has covered me all over. There is nothing exposed of my old, carnal, sinful nature. There is nothing of my past left for the devil to fasten onto. God has covered me all the way around, from head to foot, with a robe of His righteousness."

Work It Out

We receive righteousness as a gift, but we cannot leave it that way. Again, it requires a response from us—we must work out what God has worked in. Paul stated this truth very clearly in Philippians: "*Work out your salvation with fear and trembling; for it is God who is at work in you, both to will and to work for His good pleasure*" (Philippians 2:12–13 NASB). As I said above, we must work out what God has worked in. If we will not work out our righteousness, God cannot work more in. The measure of what God can work into us is the measure of what we work out.

There is a wonderful picture of the result of "outworked" righteousness in the bride of Christ as she is revealed in Revelation 19:

"Let us rejoice and be glad and give the glory to [God], for the marriage of the Lamb [Jesus] has come and His bride [the church] has made herself ready." It was given to her to clothe herself in fine linen, bright and clean; for the fine linen is the righteous acts of the saints. (Revelation 19:7–8 NASB)

In this picture, the bride has moved beyond imputed righteousness to outworked righteousness—*"the righteous acts of the saints."* This passage is a good reminder to us of the process: We do not start with righteous acts; we start with a righteousness that is imputed to us by God. After that, however, we work out what God has worked in, and that is expressed in our righteous acts. Those righteous acts will be our clothing throughout all eternity.

13

SEVENTH STAGE: GLORIFIED

In God's plan for us, He did not stop at saving us, nor did He stop at justifying us. Rather, He went on *to glorify us*. It is very important to see that *all* these stages are in the past tense. If you can believe, on the basis of Scripture, that God saved you, then you can also believe, on the basis of the Word of God, that God justified you. Accordingly, on the basis of Scripture, you can believe that God glorified you.

Glorification Is for Now

You cannot put off glorification to the future as something wonderful to look forward to. Being glorified is for us now—here, in time, during this life. Salvation leads to justification, and justification leads to glorification.

To be glorified, or to enter glorification, means to share Christ's glory with Him. Before Jesus went to the cross, when He was praying prophetically to the Father, He said of His disciples, "*The glory which You have given Me **I have given to them**"* (John 17:22 NASB). Notice that it was not *going to* happen; it *had* happened. The glory that the Father had given Jesus was made available to His disciples—and to us—through His sacrificial death and triumphant resurrection.

Let me repeat: If you enter into the fullness of God's plan, you can make these three declarations: "God saved me," "God justified me," and "God glorified me." You can use the same tense for all aspects—not the future tense but the past tense. These blessings have already happened. They are yours now.

In Romans 4, Paul explained that we are justified through the resurrection of Jesus. Paul spoke about the patriarch Abraham's faith in God and referred to the Old Testament Scripture that says, *"Abram* [Abraham] *believed the* LORD, *and he credited [*"reckoned" NASB] *it to him as righteousness"* (Genesis 15:6; see also Romans 4:20–22). Then, Paul went on to say:

> *Now not for his sake only was it written that it was credited to* [Abraham], *but for our sake also, to whom it will be credited, as those who believe in Him who raised Jesus our Lord from the dead, He who was delivered over because of our transgressions, and was raised [resurrected] because of our justification.* (Romans 4:23–25 NASB)

Jesus died to pay the penalty for our sins. But when He rose again from the dead, it was to bring us justification. When God resurrected Jesus, He reversed the verdicts of two human courts—a secular Roman court and a religious Jewish court. Both courts had declared Jesus worthy of death and had seen that He was executed. But on the third day, when the stone was rolled away—when God brought Jesus back from the dead—God overturned those two human verdicts. He declared, in effect, "This is indeed My Son. This is indeed the promised Messiah. There is no sin in Him. He is totally righteous. He cannot be held by the chains of death."

The resurrection vindicated the righteousness of Jesus. But His resurrection vindicates our righteousness, also. Our guilt was imputed to Jesus, and He died because of our guilt. When we believe in Him and His resurrection, His righteousness is then imputed to us in return. Because He was vindicated by resurrection, we are likewise vindicated, justified, and acquitted by His resurrection.

Glorified Through the Ascension of Jesus

We need to take another step, however, because God does not stop at resurrection in regard to our salvation. He takes us beyond resurrection and justification to ascension; and, through ascension, we are glorified. We are justified through the resurrection of Jesus, and we are glorified through the ascension of Jesus.

Paul made this truth clear in his letter to the Ephesians:

But God, being rich in mercy, because of His great love with which He loved us, even when we were dead in our transgressions, made us alive together with Christ (by grace you have been saved), and raised us up [resurrected us] with Him, and seated us with Him in the heavenly places in Christ Jesus.

(Ephesians 2:4–6 NASB)

God performed the following three actions on our behalf, all of which are stated in the past tense: He *"made us alive together with Christ," "raised us up* [resurrected us] *with* [Christ]," and *"seated us with Him in the heavenly places in Christ Jesus."* Jesus is sitting on the throne of God; and, if we are seated with Him, we are also sitting on the throne of God. The Weymouth translation actually renders Ephesians 2:6 as "[He] *enthroned us with Him...."*

In the previous chapter, we looked at Job's question *"How can a mortal be righteous before God?"* (Job 9:2). In the book of Job, there is also a beautiful prophetic Scripture that I am sure was not fully understood by Elihu, the man who uttered it:

[God] *does not withdraw His eyes from the righteous; but with kings on the throne He has seated them forever, and they are exalted.*   (Job 36:7 NASB)

Salvation is not just resurrection—it is also exaltation, which is glorification and enthronement. And remember, this means you, too—because you have been made righteous by faith in Jesus.

Jesus is sitting on the throne of God. If we are seated with Him, we are also sitting on God's throne.

"A Secret and Hidden Wisdom"

This amazing process of glorification that we have been examining is the secret, hidden wisdom of God that Paul spoke about in 1 Corinthians 2. He began by telling the Corinthians,

When I came to you, brethren, I did not come proclaiming to you the testimony of God in lofty words or wisdom. For I decided to know nothing among you except Jesus Christ and him crucified.   (1 Corinthians 2:1–2 RSV)

First of all, Paul laid aside all his natural, human, intellectual, academic knowledge. Then he spoke of another wisdom:

Yet among the mature we do impart wisdom, although it is not a wisdom of this age or of the rulers of this age, who are doomed to pass away. But we impart a secret and hidden wisdom of God, which God decreed before the ages for our glorification.   (1 Corinthians 2:6–7 RSV)

Before time began, God had this wonderful plan that included seven phases—of which the final phase was glorification. The last stage comes through *"a secret and hidden wisdom of God."* This revelation is not granted to the natural understanding; therefore, it cannot be learned from a book. Rather, the revelation of God's complete plan comes through the cross—through knowing *"Jesus Christ and him crucified."* The cross is the only doorway to this secret, hidden wisdom of God.

Identification Is the Key

The key to God's plan for us is identification. Jesus identified Himself with us in our guilt, and He totally paid the penalty we deserved for it. In return, when we believe in Christ, we are identified with Him in His death, His burial, His resurrection, and His ascension. When we come to His ascension, that means we enter into glory with Him. The end result of the *"secret and hidden wisdom"* is our glorification—and it is applied to our lives here and now. What you believe determines your attitudes and your lifestyle. Therefore, when you understand that you are glorified with Jesus, you are going to live a different kind of life. As Paul wrote in Colossians,

> *Since, then, you have been raised with Christ, set your hearts on things above, where Christ is seated at the right hand of God. Set your minds on things above, not on earthly things. For you died, and your life is now hidden with Christ in God. When Christ, who is your life, appears, then you also will appear with him in glory.*   (Colossians 3:1–4)

What Paul referred to here, combined with the truths we have been exploring in the previous chapters, is the place of total security in God. In Christ, you died. When Jesus died on the cross, that ended the whole of the old sinful life. You are not only raised with Him, but you are enthroned with Him, as well. *"Your life is now hidden with Christ in God."*

Can you think of a safer condition than to have a life that is hidden with Christ in God? What harm can come to you? What evil can reach you? What can Satan do against you? What limit can there be to your security when you realize that your life is hidden with Christ in God?

Simply grasp the amazing truth that *"Christ...is your life."* Those four simple words can change the whole way you face life. This is the climax of God's wonderful plan. Do not stop short of it, because it is indeed the place of total security.

14

ETERNAL HOPE

Now that we have covered all seven stages of God's plan for us, let's turn to the impact upon our lives of the security God's plan affords us. First of all, knowing God's sovereign plan for us gives us an eternal hope. *Hope* is one of the most beautiful words in any language. Hope in the heart gives us patience and strength to endure hardship, calamity, and all the other pressures that come against us in life. Hope does not allow us to bypass difficulties, but it does give us the strength to go through them.

A Refuge and a Hope

Having hope is wonderful. In contrast, having an outlook of hopelessness saps initiative, strength, and the very will to live. To be without hope in this life is tragic, and to be without hope in death is the ultimate tragedy. However, that is not the fate of the soul who is committed to Jesus.

> *When calamity comes, the wicked are brought down, but even in death the righteous have a refuge.* (Proverbs 14:32)

The King James Version translates the above verse in the following way:

> *The wicked is driven away in his wickedness: but the righteous hath hope in his death.* (Proverbs 14:32 KJV)

A powerful truth comes from this combination of the *New International Version*, which says, "*Even in death the righteous have a refuge*," and the King James Version, which reads, "*The righteous hath hope in his death.*" For the soul committed to the Lord, there is a refuge, and there is hope, even in the valley of the shadow of death.

We can contrast those beautiful words from Proverbs with what Paul wrote in Ephesians about those who do not have a relationship with Christ. He was writing to Gentile believers who had never known anything about the Lord until they heard the gospel. They had no background in the Scriptures and no past knowledge of the true God. This is what Paul said to them:

> *Remember that at that time you were separate from Christ* [cut off from Him, not related to Him], *excluded from citizenship in Israel and foreigners to the covenants of the promise, without hope and without God in the world.*
>
> (Ephesians 2:12)

These are some of the saddest, most terrible words in the Bible: "*without hope and without God in the world.*" The reason why these Ephesians had at one time been without hope is that they had been separated from Christ. The soul who is building only on the sands of time—who has never made a commitment to the eternal Rock, Jesus Christ—is without Christ, without hope, and without God.

I trust that as you read this, you will give heed to these words. If you have never taken the opportunity offered earlier to commit yourself to Christ the eternal Rock, I pray that you will resolve not to continue another day without Christ, without hope, and without God. (Please refer to the prayer of salvation in the early part of chapter 3 or at the end of chapter 11.)

For the soul committed to the Lord, there is a refuge, and there is hope, even in the valley of the shadow of death.

The Basis of Our Hope: Union with Christ

Having considered the contrast in this life between the person who is related to Christ and the person who is not related to Christ, I want to take that picture a little further. Let's look now at the contrast at death between the individual who is united to Christ by faith, and the individual who is separated from Christ. In 1 Thessalonians, Paul was writing to Christian believers who had only recently come to the Lord. He was explaining the appropriate Christian response to the death of a fellow believer. Such a death is a sorrowful occasion, he said, but it brings a kind of sorrow that is totally different from the sorrow of this world.

> *Brothers, we do not want you to be ignorant about those who fall asleep, or to grieve like the rest of men, who have no hope.*   (1 Thessalonians 4:13)

Notice that *"the rest of men"* who are not united to Christ have no hope in death. On the other hand, speaking about believers who have died, Paul used a phrase commonly found in the New Testament in such a context. Rather than saying that they had "died," he said that they had "[fallen] *asleep*." Then he went on to explain the basis for our hope:

> *We believe that Jesus died and rose again and so we believe that God will bring with Jesus those who have fallen asleep in him.*   (1 Thessalonians 4:14)

Notice also the vital phrase *"in him."* In that relationship to Christ, they have fallen asleep—but they are united by faith to the One who Himself died and rose again from the dead. This union guarantees them a similar resurrection in God's appointed hour. Paul then explains what lies ahead for those in Christ:

According to the Lord's own word, we tell you that we who are still alive, who are left till the coming of the Lord, will certainly not precede those who have fallen asleep. For the Lord himself will come down from heaven, with a loud command, with the voice of the archangel and with the trumpet call of God, and the dead in Christ will rise first. After that, we who are still alive and are left will be caught up with them in the clouds to meet the Lord in the air. And so we will be with the Lord forever. Therefore encourage each other with these words.

(1 Thessalonians 4:15–18)

These are words of encouragement for all of us who are united with Christ. We are not to grieve as others do who have no hope. If our loved one dies in Christ, we will miss him, and there will be very real pain in our heart, but it will not be a hopeless pain. We have the assurance that when Jesus returns, we will meet our loved one again, and together we will be with the Lord forever. Therefore, we are able to encourage one another with this hope.

Two Vivid Memories

In regard to this topic of hope, I want to relate two vivid scenes that I witnessed in Africa. The first took place at the pyramids at Giza in Egypt. As I was looking at the pyramids, a Muslim funeral happened to be taking place at a cemetery just about a quarter of a mile away. A large group of women, all clothed in black, were making the most terrible wailing noise of absolutely hopeless grief. The sound of their grief pierced my heart. At first, I silently prayed, *God, thank You that You've delivered us from that hopelessness at death.* Then, in the next moment, a cry went up out of my heart for the millions of people who do not know this hope at death.

The second scene took place earlier, in East Africa, where I was the principal of a training college for African teachers. One of our female students, named Agneta, had acquired typhoid fever and was in a coma. I went with my first wife, Lydia, to visit her in the hospital. Because Agneta was in a coma, she was unable to respond. I prayed silently, *Lord, let her come out of that coma long enough for me to ask her the one vital question.* Almost immediately, she opened her eyes and looked up at me. I asked her, "Agneta, do you know for sure that your soul is safe in the Lord's keeping?" She looked me full in the eyes and said, "Yes." Then she lapsed back into the coma. Even though I had no further communication with her before she went into eternity, I knew all I needed to know. I knew that she was related to Jesus with that bond that can never be broken in time or eternity.

Our Eternal Hope

As we close this chapter, let us read these beautiful words from Proverbs:

> *The path of the righteous is like the first gleam of dawn, shining ever brighter till the full light of day.*   (Proverbs 4:18)

Once you have put your foot on that path of righteousness through a commitment to the Lord, the path will grow brighter with each step you take. At the end of that path, the full brightness of noonday will be your personal reunion with the Lord when you step out of time into eternity.

When you have made it through that long, dark valley of the shadow of death, you will be in the full brightness and radiance of the Lord's presence forever. *This is the reality of eternal hope.*

15

HOPE AS A REFUGE
AND AN ANCHOR

In this chapter, as we continue with the theme of hope, we will look at two helpful pictures. True, enduring hope is a rare commodity in this world. It is so precious that it will serve us well to dwell on this topic more fully.

Hope as a Refuge

As a preacher, I have certain favorite themes, and *hope* is clearly one of them. Two beautiful pictures of hope are found in the New Testament, both of them in Hebrews 6. The first picture is that of hope as a refuge:

> *Men swear by someone greater than themselves, and the oath confirms what is said and puts an end to all argument. Because God wanted to make the unchanging nature of his purpose very clear to the heirs of what was promised, he confirmed it with an oath. God did this so that, by two unchangeable things in which it is impossible for God to lie, we who have fled to take hold of the hope offered to us may be greatly encouraged.*
> (Hebrews 6:16–18)

The writer of Hebrews assures us that our confidence in God—you might even say our security in Him—is based on two absolutely sure and unchanging foundations: First, God's Word; and, second, God's oath. Actually, it was not necessary for God to do more than give us His Word. But He was so concerned that we would have total assurance that He gave us His Word and then confirmed it with His oath. *"So that, by two unchangeable things in which it is impossible for God to lie, we who have fled to take hold of the hope offered to us may be greatly encouraged."*

When the writer said, *"We who have fled to take hold of the hope..."* he was drawing on a picture from the Old Testament. Under the old covenant, if a man was being pursued by *"an avenger of blood"* who wanted to take his life, there were *"cities of refuge"* to which he could flee and where he would be secure if he was innocent of murder or had killed someone accidentally. (See, for example, Numbers 35:14–25.) In addition, if someone fled to the altar of God and caught hold of the horns of the altar, it was not generally permissible to drag him away from that place until he was assured of a fair trial. (See 1 Kings 1:50–51.)

The writer of Hebrews compared fleeing for refuge to catch hold of the horns of the altar with our hope in God's unchanging Word and oath. When we catch hold of those "horns" and hold on to them, there is nothing that can drag us away from them. We may be pursued by our guilt, our insecurities, our fear of the future, or our fear of sickness, but if we can make it to the altar of hope and catch hold of those horns, we are safe. God's unchanging Word is the place of true and permanent security.

The concept of "fleeing to take hold of the hope" suggests urgency. It implies that the pressures are mounting, and the opposing forces are gathering against us, and we must be swift. It is urgent for us to make it to the altar before those forces sweep us away, depriving us of the opportunity God has given us.

When pressures come, I believe it is a matter of urgency for us to put our faith and our hope without reservation in the faithfulness of God and His commitment to us through Jesus Christ. It is essential that we lay hold of the security of God's Word before some calamity sweeps over us, and we are no longer able to reach out and grasp the horns of that altar of hope. Our hope in God's Word is a true refuge.

Hope as an Anchor

The writer of Hebrews gives us a second picture of hope that immediately follows the first:

> We have this hope as an anchor for the soul, firm and secure. It enters the inner sanctuary behind the curtain ["veil" NASB, NKJV, KJV], where Jesus, who went before us, has entered on our behalf. He has become a high priest forever, in the order of Melchizedek.   (Hebrews 6:19–20)

This second picture of hope is that of an "anchor for the soul." This anchor is "firm and secure" because it passes out of time through the veil that separates time and eternity. Because it reaches into the eternal realm, it is no longer subject to the pressures and changes of this temporal world. It is securely linked to the person and the work of the Lord Jesus Christ. It has been deeply and securely fastened to the Rock that never moves—Christ, the Rock of Ages.

The above passage of Scripture was one that God gave me at a time in my own experience when I desperately needed to understand the nature of hope. I have an analytical mind, and when I first read this passage, I reasoned it out in a particular way. Let me share those insights with you, because I believe they will help you.

I said to myself, So, hope is the anchor. That truth immediately gave me a picture of a boat that is secured by its anchor.

Then I asked, Why does a boat need an anchor? My answer was, Because a boat, by its very nature, floats in a totally unstable, insecure, *impermanent element—water.* You cannot grasp or lay hold of water; it just runs through your hand. There is no security there.

To achieve security in the insecure element of water, a boat must pass its anchor through the unstable element so that the anchor can grasp something stable—such as a rock or the sea bed itself.

When this picture was clear in my mind, God began to speak to me: *Your life is like that boat. You're on a sea. You're in the world in a situation that's totally unstable. There's nothing permanent— nothing you can lay hold of. There's nothing you can grasp that will give you security. If you want true and enduring security, you must do the same as a boat. You must pass the anchor of hope through the realm of time and into the realm of eternity. Only in the eternal, unchanging realm of God—His presence, His Word, the very person and nature and work of Jesus Christ—is there permanence and security.*

When I received that message from the Lord, I made a transaction with Him that changed my outlook on things. I passed my anchor right out of time and into eternity. I fastened it on the person and work of the Lord Jesus Christ. In so doing, I gained a new hope, a new peace, and a new security that have been mine ever since.

Do you desire to do the same, right now? Do you recognize your need, in the midst of all the instabilities you face, to have your anchor solidly fixed on the person and work of Jesus Christ?

If that is your desire, take a moment now to make the same transaction by means of a simple prayer and declaration:

Lord Jesus, I pass the anchor of hope for my life out of time and into Your eternal realm. I fasten the anchor of my life to the eternal work of Jesus Christ. And, by so doing, I receive Your eternal hope in my life from this point onward. Amen.

16

"THE SECRET PLACE"

In considering this theme of security, thus far we have looked primarily at the eternal, unseen realm as our only ultimate source of true and lasting security. Let us now turn our attention to various aspects of security in this present life—security during times of trouble, financial security, and emotional security. We will not only consider the various ways in which God provides these types of security, but we will also learn the conditions we must meet in order to qualify for His security in each area of our lives.

Security During Times of Trouble

First, we will look at what God's Word promises about finding security in times of trouble. In this section, I will not be speaking merely from theory but on the basis of my personal experiences. I will use these experiences as practical examples for you.

A beautiful and powerful Scripture passage that promises total security in conditions such as war, famine, pestilence, and other such circumstances is found in Psalm 91. This passage has been called "God's Atomic Bomb Shelter." Many Bible commentators attribute Psalm 91 to Moses, while others attribute it to David. Whoever the author was, either Moses or David could have written these words from personal experience of their own times of distress:

He who dwells in the shelter ["secret place" NKJV, KJV] of the Most High will rest in the shadow of the Almighty. I will say of the LORD, "He is my refuge and my fortress, my God, in whom I trust." Surely he will save you from the fowler's snare and from the deadly pestilence. He will cover you with his feathers, and under his wings you will find refuge; his faithfulness will be your shield and rampart. You will not fear the terror of night, nor the arrow that flies by day, nor the pestilence that stalks in the darkness, nor the plague that destroys at midday. A thousand may fall at your side, ten thousand at your right hand, but it will not come near you. You will only observe with your eyes and see the punishment of the wicked. If you make the Most High your dwelling—even the LORD, who is my refuge—then no harm will befall you, no disaster will come near your tent.   (Psalm 91:1–10)

Conditions for Total Security

We need to take note of the conditions for coming into the total security of which the psalmist speaks.

Dwelling in the "Secret Place"

In the *New International Version*, Psalm 91:1 reads, "*He who dwells in the shelter of the Most High….*" In the King James Version and the *New King James Version*, the word "*shelter*" is translated "*secret place*." I believe "*secret place*" is an excellent translation, because the root meaning of the Hebrew word is "a secret." Therefore, I prefer to read the verse in this way: "He who dwells in the secret place of the Most High will rest in the shadow of the Almighty."

"*Dwells*" speaks of someone who has a continuing position in God, rather than someone who merely runs into the secret place in a time of crisis. The psalm therefore depicts someone whose dwelling—whose permanent, abiding situation—is in the secret place of the Most High.

The Hebrew word translated "*rest*" is frequently used of spending the night. Therefore, the psalm would suggest that, during the hours of darkness, we will have a place of complete protection.

Making a Bold Personal Confession

A second condition for security is found in Psalm 91:2: "*I will say of the* LORD, '*He is my refuge and my fortress....*'" The psalmist declared what he believed about God. So, this second essential condition is making a bold, personal confession of one's faith in God and one's relationship to Him.

As we noted earlier in this book, we must not merely believe in our hearts, but we must also say with our mouths what we believe. "*Let the redeemed of the* LORD *say so, whom He has redeemed from the hand of the enemy*" (Psalm 107:2 NKJV). Redemption is not effective until we speak it, making it effective by our own personal confession.

We must not merely believe in our hearts, but we must also say with our mouths what we believe.

Having understood the conditions that must be met, let us now consider the various forms of trouble against which protection is promised in Psalm 91: "*the fowler's snare,*" "*the deadly pestilence,*" "*the terror of night,*" "*the arrow that flies by day,*" "*the pestilence that stalks in the darkness,*" and "*the plague that destroys at midday.*" Then, we are guaranteed protection against anything that lays men low: "*A thousand may fall at your side, ten thousand at your right hand, but it will not come near you.*"

My Experiences with God's Protection

To confirm what I have been saying about the secret place of the Most High, I want to briefly present some of my own experiences. I personally witnessed this protection of total security as a British soldier in the desert of North Africa during World War II. One day, when the German forces were raining down bombs on our area, I was sitting calmly in the middle of the desert—watching the bombs fall in a ring all around me. Not a single bomb came near me. While I was sitting there, these words came to me so clearly: *"A thousand may fall at your side, ten thousand at your right hand, but it will not come near you."* It was clear to me that God was my personal Refuge and Fortress.

During the birth of the State of Israel in 1948, I was living in Jerusalem with my first wife, Lydia, and the eight girls we had adopted. At that time, we witnessed many of the perils that are described in Psalm 91. Because of the conflict between the Jews and the surrounding Arab nations, there was a desperate shortage of food and water among the whole Jewish population. Yet, in a sovereign way, God continually provided us with sufficient food and water.

When the war actually broke out in Jerusalem, there was continual danger from artillery shelling and sniper fire in the streets. One day, our eldest daughter, Tikva, was crossing the street, and a person walking beside her was shot down. The person right next to her in the street perished, but she was protected.

Because the house in Jerusalem where we were living was less than a quarter of a mile from the front line of the battle, we lived for about six weeks in the laundry room below the basement. When we emerged, we discovered that over one hundred fifty window panes in our house had been broken by bullets. On another occasion, a bullet ricocheted into a room of our house where we were sitting. The bullet just slithered down Lydia's leg, but it did her no harm.

When I teach about "the secret place of the Most High," I am not offering just a theory. His "hiding place" is something I have experienced and proved.

17

THE DOOR TO THE
SECRET PLACE

Let us continue to examine the ways in which we discover God's security for us when we meet His conditions. In considering "the secret place of the Most High," which we discussed in the previous chapter, a question arises: How can we enter into the secret place of the Most High and make our dwelling there?

Obviously, a secret place is hidden. It is not advertised. There is no sign hanging out front telling us that this is the secret place. (If there were such a sign, it would not be a secret place anymore!) So, this secret place must be searched for and found.

Finding the Secret Place

There are some beautiful words in the book of Job that I believe relate to finding this secret place. Job asked, *"But where can wisdom be found?"* (Job 28:12). Please remember what we learned earlier: It is the wisdom of God's Word that offers us total security. (See Proverbs 1:33.)

Job pondered just where God had hidden the secret place of wisdom: *"The deep says, 'It is not in me'; the sea says, 'It is not with me'"* (Job 28:14). The secret place is not hidden somewhere in the depths of the sea. In addition, no animal, bird, or beast knows the way to it:

It is hidden from the eyes of every living thing, concealed even from the birds of the air. Destruction and Death say, "Only a rumor of it has reached our ears." God understands the way to it and he alone knows where it dwells.   (Job 28:21–23)

Most of us are familiar with stories of old castles with secret doors that opened to hidden passageways. Usually, this secret door was covered by something like a tapestry or a large portrait. Behind this covering, there was generally some little device that had to be pressed for the door to swing open, revealing the secret passage. To me, this is a picture of the entrance to the secret place of God. It is covered by a picture that we would not normally associate with it. I believe that covering is the cross of Jesus.

The Cross Opens the Way

At first, when we see the cross, we recoil from it. We don't like it, and we don't want it. But behind the cross is the door to this secret place. The cross of Jesus is the way to the secret place that no animal can find, no bird can see, and the whole of natural creation does not know about. This is because it is found in the spiritual realm, not in the natural realm.

Let us read once more the words of Paul in Colossians 3:

Since, then, you have been raised with Christ, set your hearts on things above, where Christ is seated at the right hand of God. Set your minds on things above, not on earthly things. For you died, and your life is now hidden with Christ in God. When Christ, who is your life, appears, then you also will appear with him in glory.   (Colossians 3:1–4)

Notice again these key words: "…*your life is now hidden with Christ in God.*" This is not a truth merely for the next world. It is true right now! To be hidden with Christ in God is to dwell in the secret place.

Paul said, "*You died....*" That is the cross. The secret is that, when Jesus died, He did not die only for Himself. He died for us as our Representative. He took our guilt and our condemnation by paying our penalty and dying our death. When we understand this reality and, by faith, receive what Scripture says, we realize that when Jesus died, *we died with Him*. Paul reiterated this truth in Galatians, where he said, "*I have been crucified with Christ and I no longer live, but Christ lives in me*" (Galatians 2:20).

Paul was saying to the Colossians, and to us, "*You died....*" When you died with Christ, you passed through death—through the death of Jesus on the cross—into a new realm. Again, this realm is not in the natural world. It is a realm that the senses cannot discern—a realm that we as natural creatures do not perceive. The secret place is a realm in Christ where we are hidden with Christ in God.

---

*The secret place is found in the spiritual realm,
not in the natural realm.*

"Hidden with Christ in God"

Pause for a moment to consider the total security that is represented by our being "*hidden with Christ in God.*" In this place of hiddenness, you have, as it were, a double protection: You are in Christ, and you are in God. Therefore, nothing in the entire universe can reach you unless it first comes through God and through Christ.

Our true life is not in this visible world. We are here in the flesh, but we have another kind of life—a different life from a different Source. Our body is just a clay vessel that this life currently inhabits. Paul said our clay vessel may go through many difficulties and pressures; there is no guarantee that we will not face them. But, in that clay vessel is an eternal life—an incorruptible, indestructible life that is so totally identified with God and with Jesus Christ that nothing can ever happen to us unless it is in the will of God and of Christ. (See 2 Corinthians 4:7–10, 16–18.)

This is total security. It is security in the midst of war, famine, pestilence, or earthquake. No matter what comes, we are in Christ—in that secret place of the Most High. We are protected from all harm and all danger. And the door to that secret place of protection, safety, and security is the cross.

18

PROTECTION AGAINST FEAR AND WORRY

We turn now to another area of security that we all need but, alas, do not all experience—*emotional security*. Mental and emotional pressures are increasing due to our contemporary lifestyle. I once read an estimate that, in a normal lifetime, one out of every four persons in the United States will need some kind of psychiatric help. That is a staggering figure. The result is that most psychiatric hospitals today are filled to overflowing.

When a person comes to need psychiatric help, that person has succumbed in some way to mental or emotional pressures. It is estimated that for every person who actually recognizes his need and seeks psychiatric help, there are probably twice as many people who do not recognize their need or seek help, even though, to some degree, they have the same type of problem.

The Remedy

The remedy for mental and emotional pressures could be summed up in one word: *peace*. I refer to peace not in the connotation of the absence of war, but in the sense of personal fulfillment, completeness, and rest.

There are two primary enemies of peace: *fear* and *worry*. Each of them comes in many different forms. For example, we may fear or worry about sickness, or other people's opinions, or a financial downturn. Fear is like a dagger that is thrust into us, while worry is like a little nagging worm that eats away at us. Yet, in the end, each of these assailants is destructive.

God's primary protection against fear and worry is *trust*. The prophet Isaiah said,

> You [addressing the Lord] *will keep in perfect peace him whose mind is steadfast, because he trusts in you. Trust in the* LORD *forever, for the* LORD, *the* LORD, *is the Rock eternal.*
>
> (Isaiah 26:3–4)

"*You will keep in perfect peace*"—that is complete protection against fear and worry.

The above passage also speaks about the area where fear and worry attack—the mind. "*You will keep in perfect peace **him whose mind is steadfast….**" The way to have a settled, steadfast mind is stated in the next phrase: "*…because he trusts in you.*" Then follows this beautiful exhortation: "*Trust in the* LORD *forever, for the* LORD, *the* LORD, *is the Rock eternal.*"

This description of the Lord echoes our earlier study of Hebrews 6:19, where we considered the anchor of the soul that passes out of time into eternity, fastening onto the Lord, the Rock of Ages. The above passage gives yet another picture of the eternal Rock.

Steps to Achieving Trust

As a follow-up to the trust factor that Isaiah introduced to us, let us look at two steps to achieving trust.

1. Be Renewed in the Spirit of Your Mind

The first is to "*be renewed in the spirit of your mind*" (Ephesians 4:23 NASB, NKJV, KJV). Our minds are ultimately motivated, directed, and controlled by spiritual forces. Therefore, to enter into real trust, we must have a Spirit controlling our minds that is different from the spirit that controls the minds of the people of this world.

We must let another Spirit take charge of our minds—reprogramming our thinking and giving us new thought patterns and objectives that are aligned with Christ's. Paul contrasted the spirit that operates in the people of the world with the kind of spirit that should be operating in a child of God:

> *God did not give us a spirit of timidity* ["*fear*" NKJV, KJV, or cowardice], *but a spirit of power, of love and of self-discipline.*　　　　　　　　　　　　　　　　　(2 Timothy 1:7)

The *"spirit of power, of love and of self-discipline"* to which Paul referred is, of course, the Holy Spirit. He is the Spirit we must invite to control our minds. When the Holy Spirit comes in, He excludes the spirit of timidity, or fear.

We must allow the Holy Spirit to reprogram
our thinking and give us new thought patterns
and objectives that are aligned with Christ's.

---

2. Focus on the Positive

The second step to achieving trust in our minds is to focus on the positive. We recognize this truth in the following passage written by Paul to the Philippians:

> *Do not be anxious about anything, but in everything, by prayer and petition, with thanksgiving, present your requests to God. And the peace of God, which transcends all understanding, will guard your hearts and your minds in Christ Jesus.*
>　　　　　　　　　　　　　　　　　(Philippians 4:6–7)

Never try to reason out the peace of God, because it *"transcends all understanding."* His peace is something that goes beyond our power to reason out. So, how do we experience it? We just receive it from Him.

In the next verse, Paul prescribed how to retain the peace of God:

> *Finally, brothers, whatever is true, whatever is noble, whatever is right, whatever is pure, whatever is lovely, whatever is admirable—if anything is excellent or praiseworthy—think about such things.*   (Philippians 4:8)

What Paul described here is the ongoing recipe for peace: Focus on the positive. Don't focus on the people who have harmed you. Don't focus on the problems that may arise. Don't focus on what is evil. Focus on what is good. Focus on God, His love, and His faithfulness. Focus on the Word of God. Focus on the people who care for you and pray for you. Think about all the good that you have received from people. Never let your mind be preoccupied with the negative.

Years ago, when I was serving with the British forces in Egypt, somebody pointed out to me that there are basically two kinds of birds of prey. There are those that kill their prey and eat it alive, and there are those that feed on rotten meat that stinks. That person said to me, "Both birds find what they're looking for!" Our minds are like that. If we want to feed on rotten meat, we can do that. But if we want to feed on what is fresh, we can do that. *We make the decision.*

When Fear Comes

I want to point out that the Bible is very realistic. It never assumes that its recipe for peace will be applied with complete success the first time. It leaves room for an ongoing tension between fear and trust. I'm sure each of us can identify with that situation, because most of us experience it at times. King David wrote,

> [God,] *when I am afraid, I will put my trust in You. In God, whose word I praise, in God I have put my trust; I shall not be afraid. What can mere man do to me?*
>
> (Psalm 56:3–4 NASB)

Please note that David did not say he would never be afraid. Instead, he said, in effect, "When I am afraid, I will not yield to fear. I will not focus on fear or let fear dominate my thinking. Rather, I will turn away from my fear. I will look to the Lord, and I will put my trust in Him."

In the same way, as we turn to the Lord and put our trust in Him, we must honor His Word—because it is the expression of God's will, counsel, and attitude toward us. Circumstances might seem to suggest that God does not care about us, that He is far away, and that our situation is not under His control. But when we put our trust in Him and His Word, we choose not to believe those lies of Satan.

When fear comes, the remedy is not to say, "I'm not afraid." Instead, we say, "I won't yield to fear. I won't focus on fear. I will turn to God. I will put my trust in Him and in His Word, which never changes. Because I trust in God and His Word, fear cannot take hold of me."

Are you facing a situation right now that is bringing fear into your heart? Why not repeat the remedy for fear out loud as your declaration of trust in God?

> I won't yield to fear. I won't focus on fear. I will turn to God. I will put my trust in Him and in His Word, which never changes. Because I trust in God and His Word, fear cannot take hold of me. Amen.

19

PROTECTION AGAINST DISCOURAGEMENT AND DEPRESSION

In the previous chapter, we discussed two enemies of emotional security that arise to challenge us—fear and worry. There are two additional enemies that attempt to keep us from true emotional security: *discouragement* and *depression*. Having been invited to teach and preach in many countries, I have had the opportunity to ask congregations all around the world what battles they frequently face. In those years of informally surveying Christian audiences, I have found that discouragement and depression are two of the commonest enemies of God's people. In dealing with discouragement and depression, just as with fear and worry, it is first of all a question of what spirit controls our minds.

Listen to the Encourager

To reaffirm which spirit should be in control of our minds, let's look at a passage from the gospel of John. This is one aspect of what Jesus said to His disciples as He was about to leave them to return to the Father in heaven:

> I will ask the Father, and he will give you another Counselor
> to be with you forever—the Spirit of truth. (John 14:16–17)

The Greek word translated *"Counselor"* in the above verse has also been translated several different ways in English, such as *"Helper"* (NASB, NKJV) and *"Comforter"* (KJV). Another word that could also be used is "Encourager." The last term is one of my favorites, because, in modern English, the phrase "to comfort" also means "to encourage."

I want to emphasize one fact very clearly and firmly: *The Holy Spirit never discourages the people of God.* He is the Encourager, not the discourager. Any spirit that works in your mind to discourage you is not the Holy Spirit! You need to be renewed in the spirit of your mind and make room for the Encourager.

Discern Truth from Lies

Jesus said that the Holy Spirit, the Encourager, is *"the Spirit of truth."* One of the ways the Holy Spirit encourages us is by bringing us the truth. Satan is a liar, and he discourages us by bringing us lies. There is a spiritual battle being waged over our minds, and we need to respond to the right source. Some Christians find themselves in a state of mental confusion due to this battle. Sometimes, they listen to the Holy Spirit bringing them the truth. But, other times, they are caught off guard and listen to the enemy bringing his lies and discouragement.

One good way to discern the difference between what is true and what is a lie is the reality I have just pointed out—one that needs to be emphasized again: *The Holy Spirit never discourages the people of God.* God's Spirit may rebuke us or convict us, but He never discourages us. Our ultimate input from the Holy Spirit is always positive, never negative.

Let me reassure you: If there ever is some force in your mind saying that you are no good, that you will never make it, that you will never know victory, that you are a failure, or that God has given up on you, it is not the Holy Spirit speaking to you. It is not the truth. It is a lie! Please remember that the Holy Spirit comes with the truth. The devil comes with lies like the ones listed above.

A little further on in John's gospel, Jesus prayed to the Father, *"Your word is truth"* (John 17:17). If we put together these two thoughts—this verse from John 17 and the passage from John 14 that we examined above—we find that the Holy Spirit encourages us by bringing to our minds the truth of God's Word. As we have seen, the truth of God's Word for a child of God is ultimately always positive and always encouraging. In particular, the Holy Spirit shows us where to find protection when we are assailed by discouragement and depression. Where is that protection? It is, of course, in the Word of God.

God's Spirit may rebuke us or convict us,
but He never discourages us.

Safeguard Yourself Against Depression

A beautiful verse that is very precious to me is Isaiah 61:3, where the Scriptures say that God will give us *"the garment of praise for* [in place of] *the spirit of heaviness"* (NKJV, KJV). *"The spirit of heaviness"* is depression. When the spirit of heaviness, or depression, assails us, God has provided a remedy to keep that spirit away from us—it is *"the garment of praise."* When we put on the garment of praise and begin to praise and worship God, then that spirit of heaviness, or depression, cannot get at us. It is defeated.

The garment of praise surrounds us and protects our whole being against that spirit of heaviness. The best course of action is to live with the garment continually wrapped around us. A person who is always praising God does not have time to be discouraged or depressed. Anytime the spirit of heaviness comes to you, remember to put on the garment of praise.

In the New Testament, Paul shared with us two other items of protection against discouragement and depression:

> *Since we belong to the day, let us be self-controlled, putting on faith and love as a breastplate, and the hope of salvation as a helmet.*   (1 Thessalonians 5:8)

The first item of protection is the *"breastplate"* of *"faith and love,"* worn over the area of the heart. So, the heart is protected by faith and love. The second is the *"helmet"* of *"the hope of salvation,"* which protects the mind. Specifically, it is a helmet of hope. When our minds are being assailed, we need to put on that helmet of hope, not only by refusing to give way to despair, but also by refusing to entertain the negative. We then allow the Holy Spirit to show us all the glorious and positive truths from the Word of God upon which we can base a strong, steadfast, confident hope. As with the garment of praise, when our minds are filled with hope, there is no room for depression or discouragement.

My Battle with Depression

The reality of these defenses against discouragement is very vivid for me. When I was a young preacher, I had a tremendous battle against depression for many years. In various aspects of the ministry, I was quite successful. Yet I never succeeded in dealing with this problem of depression. It was something that would come over me like a dark gray mist, coming down over my head and my shoulders until I felt like I was enshrouded under it. It would shut me off from my wife, from my other family members, and from the members of my congregation. I would feel as if I were shut up in that gray mist of hopelessness, giving me the sense that I would never make it. It was as if something was saying to me, "You've come as far as you can come, and you'll never get any farther. Others can, but you can't."

I would regularly struggle against this overwhelming presence for many, many hours, doing everything I knew to do. I prayed, I fasted, and I read the Bible, but somehow I never got permanent victory over it. One day, as I was reading the Bible, I came to the verse in Isaiah that we just noted, which says that God will give us *"the garment of praise for* [in place of] *the spirit of heaviness."* When I read the words *"the spirit of heaviness,"* something jumped inside me. I said to myself, *That's your problem!*

In that moment, I realized by revelation from Scripture that I was not dealing with just a mental attitude. It was not just something psychological. Rather, I was battling a personal enemy—an invisible being in the spirit world—called a "spirit of heaviness." A spirit of depression had been systematically assailing my mind. When I realized I was dealing with this invisible being, this spirit of heaviness, I was 80 percent of the way to reaching the solution to my problem. To complete the circuit, I needed only one other Scripture. And I found it in the book of Joel: *"Whoever calls on the name of the* LORD *will be delivered"* (Joel 2:32 NASB). Immediately, I called upon the name of the Lord, and He graciously set me free from that spirit of heaviness. Then, the Holy Spirit showed me that, to stay free, I had to take the same steps that I have been recommending to you.

First, I had to put on the garment of praise.

Second, I had to stop using negative talk, no longer being a grumbler and expressing all types of fears and worries and anxieties.

Furthermore, every time I was confronted with a problem, I had to search the Scriptures for the solution to that problem, boldly quoting the answer and giving praise and thanks to God for the solution. I could no longer afford to be a pessimist. For me, pessimism was a sure way to defeat.

This was the very personal lesson the Lord gave me. By wearing the garment of praise and the helmet of hope, I came to a place of total security against those evil forces of discouragement and depression.[2]

If you are facing a similar battle, fight back with the following declaration of faith:

> Father, in the face of the assailants of discouragement and depression, I make these declarations:
>
> + You have given me, at Jesus' request, the Holy Spirit. He is with me forever—helping me, comforting me, encouraging me, and bringing the truth of Your Word to me. Thank You that His truth is always positive, always encouraging.
>
> + You have given me the garment of praise in place of the spirit of heaviness. I praise You, Lord, for Your great faithfulness to me. I also take up the breastplate of faith and love, protecting my heart, and the helmet of hope, protecting my mind.
>
> In the name of Jesus, I renounce and reject the spirit of heaviness that assails me, and I wrap myself in the garment of praise. I call upon the name of Jesus to deliver me from any spirit of heaviness. I declare that my speech will overflow with the promises of God's Word—speaking blessings, encouragement, praises to God, and expressions of hope.
>
> The Lord is my Deliverer, my Hope forever, and my eternal Source of total security. Amen.

---

2. For further study on the topic of hope, see *The Helmet of Hope*, available through Derek Prince Ministries, which unfolds Derek's personal experience in greater detail.

20

PROTECTION AGAINST CRITICISM AND MISREPRESENTATION

In the last several chapters, we have been focusing on the quest for emotional security. Two of the most vicious enemies of emotional security are *criticism* and *misrepresentation*. A main weapon Satan uses against God's people is the tongue.

The enemy's very name in the New Testament, *"the devil,"* means "the slanderer." That is his nature. He is the slanderer and the accuser. Very often, he will influence human tongues to be used against believers in Jesus. He does not come to us in person. Instead, he secretly, invisibly, takes control of human tongues and turns them against God's people—using the words of others to slander, to accuse, to criticize, and to misrepresent.

When Satan Attacks Us Through Others

Jeremiah the prophet understood what it means to be criticized and misrepresented. It was revealed to him that his enemies were saying, *"Come, let's make plans against Jeremiah....Let's attack him with our tongues..."* (Jeremiah 18:18). At one time or another, Satan attacks most of the Lord's servants in this way. When we are attacked by the words of others, our main challenge is in how we react and respond. It is extremely important that we respond in the way the Scriptures direct. Jesus Himself spoke particularly about our response to such attacks in His Sermon on the Mount:

> *Blessed are you when people insult you, persecute you and falsely say all kinds of evil against you because of me. Rejoice and be glad, because great is your reward in heaven, for in the same way they persecuted the prophets who were before you.*
>
> (Matthew 5:11–12)

Let us further examine how we should respond to criticism and misrepresentation by exploring two important lessons: (1) criticism is a blessing, and (2) we are *"hidden with Christ in God"* (Colossians 3:3).

Lesson #1: Criticism Is a Blessing

When we are maligned because of our faith in Jesus, it is a blessing. However, if we are criticized because of our own error or wrong conduct, then it isn't necessarily a blessing. But when we are criticized and attacked because of our relationship and commitment to Jesus Christ, then Jesus says, *"Blessed are you."*

So, if people attack us with unjust criticism or slander, we must not regard it as a problem to lament over. When we understand what Jesus was saying in Matthew 5, we can see that our enemies are really doing us a favor. They may not realize it, but they are actually piling up rewards for us in heaven. So, how should we respond to such critics? We shouldn't try to stop them. We should let them go on, because the longer they go on, the greater our reward in heaven!

Furthermore, Jesus told us that when such criticism comes, we are in very good company, because that is the way the prophets were treated. As we just saw, that is how the prophet Jeremiah was treated. Consequently, when people attack you with their tongues because of your relationship with the Lord, you are in the tradition of the prophets. *"Rejoice and be glad,"* because you are going to earn a great reward in heaven. Therefore, a major protection against criticism is to have the right response.

Lesson #2: We Are "Hidden with Christ in God"

Second, we need to remember that we are in Christ. The secret, hidden place is the place in Christ that Paul wrote about: *"For you died, and your life is now hidden with Christ in God"* (Colossians 3:3). When we are hidden with Christ, we are covered by His righteousness. That is a most beautiful thought, if only we can grasp it.

Isaiah declared, *"My God...has clothed me with garments of salvation and arrayed me in a robe of righteousness"* (Isaiah 61:10). Another Bible version says it this way: *"...He has wrapped me with a robe of righteousness"* (Isaiah 61:10 NASB). Once we enter into God's salvation, we have a robe of righteousness—not our own righteousness but Christ's righteousness, which we received by faith. We are totally covered with the righteousness of Christ. All the weak points in our character and conduct are covered by that robe.

Regarding our righteousness in Christ, Paul wrote,

God made him who had no sin [Jesus] to be sin for us, so that in him we might become the righteousness of God.

(2 Corinthians 5:21)

Notice the words *"in him."* All our righteousness is dependent upon our relationship with Jesus. When we are in Him, we are in the secret place. And when we are in the secret place, we are covered by the righteousness of God in Christ. Therefore, when people criticize and attack us on the basis of our relationship with

Jesus, they are not criticizing our righteousness. They are criticizing Christ's righteousness.

When we are wrapped in the righteousness of Christ, we are protected, so we need not try to stand on our own righteousness. We need not try to answer for ourselves. Why? Because when people attack the righteousness of Jesus that is wrapped around us, God the Father Himself moves in and deals with them.

This principle was stated clearly by the prophet Isaiah:

> *"No weapon forged against you will prevail, and you will refute every tongue that accuses you. This is the heritage of the servants of the* LORD, *and this is their vindication from me,"* declares the LORD. (Isaiah 54:17)

When people attack God's righteousness, it is God who vindicates. An alternative translation for *"vindication"* in the above verse is "righteousness." Therefore, the verse could be translated, "'...their righteousness is from me,' declares the Lord." (See, for example, NKJV.)

This is why no weapon crafted against us can prevail. This is why we can refute every tongue that criticizes or attacks us. It is because we are not facing our accusers in our own righteousness. We are hidden in the secret place in Christ. We are wrapped with the robe of His righteousness. Again, when we are attacked by people's criticisms, or when we face slander and misrepresentation, it is really a blessing in disguise. Why? Because it drives us once more into the secret place—the place of total security.

When we are wrapped in the righteousness of Christ,
we are protected, so we need not try to
stand on our own righteousness.

Let's take a moment to consider what King David said about that secret place of total security. In Psalm 31, he spoke about the relationship of the Lord to His servants: *"You hide them in the secret place of Your presence from the conspiracies of man; You keep them secretly in a shelter from the strife of tongues"* (Psalm 31:20 NASB).

David was very familiar with human conspiracies and the attacks of people's tongues. His refuge was the same as the one expressed in Psalm 91:1: *"The secret place of the Most High"* (NKJV).

Please notice the emphasis on being hidden and being secret. We must not expose ourselves. Instead, we must take refuge in Christ's righteousness. The moment we begin to expose ourselves—the moment we start to fight back using the same weapons the enemy uses, or the moment we try to justify ourselves—we have moved out of the secret place without realizing it. By so doing, we have actually lost our cover and our protection. The remedy for criticism and misrepresentation is to stay hidden in the secret place, covered with the robe of Christ's righteousness. We must never try to meet people's criticisms in our own righteousness.

It is important that you learn to respond appropriately to all the pressures I have highlighted in the last several chapters: fear and worry, discouragement and depression, and criticism and misrepresentation. React in the right way. *Let them do you good.* Let them serve God's purposes in your life.

Every time you encounter these pressures, let them drive you back into the secret place. That is why God allows them to come. He wants to bring you to the place where you are dwelling in the secret place of the Most High—a place of total emotional security.

In our next chapter, we will move on from this area of emotional security to one of the commonest areas where people crave security—the financial realm.

21

FINANCIAL SECURITY

In all periods of human history, people have been concerned about security in the realm of finances and material possessions. In recent years, the pressures of worldwide economic instability have greatly increased this concern and have made it continually difficult for people to find satisfactory forms of investment. One very obvious result has been the dramatic increase in the value of gold, silver, precious stones, and other collector's items. People are investing in these areas because they do not feel secure about many other traditional forms of investment.

I know of a wealthy Arabic man from an oil-producing nation who feels secure only if he has a hundred million dollars available in ready cash. If he doesn't have that amount of money accessible, he cannot sleep at night. In order to keep that sum available, he has deposited a hundred million dollars in a Swiss bank account, and he pays the bank a 3-percent commission to look after his money. In other words, it costs him three million dollars a year to keep his hundred million dollars secure. That is his concept of security. Yet, as much as anyone might like to think so, investments of this kind do not bring true or permanent security.

A Permanent and Secure Investment

There is an alternative type of investment that is permanent and completely secure. In His Sermon on the Mount, Jesus said,

*Do not store up for yourselves treasures on earth, where moth
and rust destroy, and where thieves break in and steal. But
store up for yourselves treasures in heaven, where neither moth
nor rust destroys, and where thieves do not break in or steal;
for where your treasure is, there your heart will be also.*

(Matthew 6:19–21 NASB)

Think of that Arabic man who has his money stowed away
in a Swiss bank. If Switzerland were to be invaded by a foreign
power, and its banking system were to be taken over, that man
would not be able to sleep. His treasure—the place where his heart
is—would be gone!

Jesus warned us that there is no place of total security in this
world system, including its banks. Consequently, He said, in effect,
"Don't invest everything in a place that isn't really secure. That is
very unwise and impractical. Invest in something that's guaranteed,
that's secure, that cannot be taken over by an alien government." The
"bank" Jesus was talking about cannot be broken into, nor can its
bullion be stolen. It is up to us to invest in the kingdom of God. It is
incumbent upon us to invest in heaven and in the purposes of God.

The Right Priority

Further on in Matthew 6, Jesus concluded,

*Do not worry then, saying, "What will we eat?" or "What
will we drink?" or "What will we wear for clothing?" For the
Gentiles eagerly seek all these things; for your heavenly Father
knows that you need all these things. But seek first His kingdom and His righteousness, and all these things will be added
to you. So do not worry about tomorrow; for tomorrow will
care for itself. Each day has enough trouble of its own.*

(Matthew 6:31–34 NASB)

It has always blessed me to realize that God knows exactly what I need, even without my ever reminding Him. When I meet His condition—to seek His kingdom first—He will take care of the rest. In essence, it is a question of the right priority. If I give proper priority to the kingdom of God and to the work of the kingdom, God will take care of me in return.

Do you agree with Jesus' statement that *"each day has enough trouble of its own"*? Jesus was a realist. He was saying, in essence, "Don't spoil today by worrying about tomorrow's problems." On the basis of several decades of experience, I can personally testify that the approach Jesus recommended really works! I have sought the kingdom of God, and God has faithfully cared for me and provided for me and my very large family.

When I meet God's condition—to seek His kingdom first—He will take care of the rest.

Paul compared placing a priority on investing in God's kingdom to sowing crops generously. He wrote, in regard to giving money,

> Remember this: Whoever sows sparingly will also reap sparingly, and whoever sows generously will also reap generously. Each man should give what he has decided in his heart to give, not reluctantly or under compulsion, for God loves a cheerful giver. And God is able to make all grace abound to you, so that in all things at all times, having all that you need, you will abound in every good work.   (2 Corinthians 9:6–8)

In the kingdom of God, there is total financial security: *"in all things," "at all times," "having all that you need," "you will abound in every [all] good work."* If we sow into the kingdom of God, then from the kingdom of God we will reap in proportion to what we have sown.

God's Unshakable Kingdom

I want to point out the contrast between the kingdom of God, in which we are invited to invest, and the kingdoms of this world. The following Scripture passage highlights this contrast:

> *At that time* [the time when God spoke to Moses on Mount Sinai] *his voice shook the earth, but now he has promised, "Once more I will shake not only the earth but also the heavens." The words "once more" indicate the removing of what can be shaken—that is, created things* [earthly kingdoms]— *so that what cannot be shaken may remain. Therefore, since we are receiving a kingdom that cannot be shaken, let us be thankful, and so worship God acceptably with reverence and awe.*   (Hebrews 12:26–28)

We are presented with two alternatives in this passage. We can invest in kingdoms, systems, and institutions of this world, which God has told us are all going to be shaken, or we can rely upon God's unshakable kingdom. In recent years, we have seen many institutions shaken. Many establishments that were regarded as sound and reliable have proved to be insecure.

We are being reminded of a great truth—that we have an alternative to what can be shaken. Rather than investing in the kingdoms of this world, we can invest in the kingdom of God. Why is that better? Because all that is invested in the kingdoms of this world will ultimately be insecure.

Isaiah gave us a vivid picture of what will happen in the earth when God shakes all the kingdoms of this world:

> *In that day men will throw away to the rodents and bats their*
> *idols of silver and idols of gold, which they made to worship.*
> *They will flee to caverns in the rocks and to the overhanging*
> *crags from dread of the LORD and the splendor of his majesty,*
> *when He rises to shake the earth.*   (Isaiah 2:20–21)

In that moment—when everything that can be shaken is shaken—people will realize they have invested in the wrong place. They will take all their gold and silver, in which they have trusted for their security, and, in contempt and disgust, they will throw it away to the rodents and the bats, because it will have no power to save them.

Therefore, if we follow the wisdom of God, we will invest in God's kingdom—not in something that is ultimately insecure. When we do what God recommends, God accepts responsibility for us in return. He guarantees that our investments will never perish. There will never be a time when the system we have been investing in will collapse, causing us to lose our assets. *Our investment is guaranteed.*

Would you like to take a moment right now to commit your finances to what is unshakable? If you have never turned your finances and your investments completely over to the Lord, now would be an appropriate time to do so.

If that is your desire, simply let the Lord know with this brief declaration:

> Lord, all that I have—all that I own in the way of possessions, resources, and investments—I now commit fully to You. I move all my assets into the kingdom of God, which cannot be shaken. They now *belong* to You, Lord. Amen.

22

GOD'S SOCIAL SECURITY

Now that you have made that very important transaction of transferring your resources into God's hands, let us deal with another aspect of financial and material security—one that I call "God's social security." As I wrote in the introduction to this book, a program of social security provided by a government for its citizens has become an accepted feature of most social systems in the Western world. In fact, people today talk about "cradle-to-grave" security. The basic concept is that you pay taxes to your government—often considerable sums of money—out of what you have earned. In turn, the government accepts responsibility for you in your time of need. Perhaps you become sick, lose your job, or come to a place in life where you are unable to work. At these points, the government takes care of you. That's called "social security."

Unfortunately, social security as we know it has been steadily eroded by inflation and other factors. Already, there are senior citizens who have invested in the government but who are not getting an adequate return on their investment—not enough to support them in comfort and honor in their old age. This is just one example of the *insecurity* of investing in a human system. I am not expressing an opposition to social security. I am simply pointing out that its "security" is strictly limited.

A Different Basis for Security

Let's face it—the need for financial and material security is real. But God offers us this security on a different basis. The basis on which He offers it is very simple: It is spiritual, and it is *established on faith*. It is founded on faith that works by love. (See Galatians 5:6 KJV.) That is the real and true basis of security in financial and material things. It is through faith in God and His Word that is expressed by acts of love toward God and toward those whom God puts in our pathway to help.

Psalm 112 gives us a picture of the person who is righteous by God's standards. I have selected some verses from this psalm to highlight, and I want to point out that the emphasis here is really on doing good to the poor and helping those in need. This is an essential part of the biblical picture of righteousness. Unfortunately, I think it has dropped out of the thinking of many contemporary Christians and churches—but it has never dropped out of the Bible.

> *Blessed is the man who fears the LORD, who finds great delight in his commands. His children will be mighty in the land; the generation of the upright will be blessed. Wealth and riches are in his house, and his righteousness endures forever.*
> (Psalm 112:1–3)

> *Good will come to him who is generous and lends freely, who conducts his affairs with justice. Surely he will never be shaken.* (Psalm 112:5–6)

> *His heart is secure, he will have no fear; in the end he will look in triumph on his foes. He has scattered abroad his gifts to the poor, his righteousness endures forever.* (Psalm 112:8–9)

Notice the direct connection between righteousness and giving to the poor. Because this man has *"scattered abroad his gifts to the poor,"* his righteousness will endure forever—and God will take total responsibility for that man's well-being. The emphasis is on generosity, on lending and giving. God promises that the person who practices this kind of generosity will not be shaken. His heart will be secure, and he will have no fear. That is true security!

The basis on which God offers financial and material security is very simple: It is spiritual, and it is established on faith.

"Lending" to the Lord

The very basic principle of "lending" to the Lord is emphasized throughout the Scriptures. Consider this verse from Proverbs:

He who has pity on the poor lends to the LORD, and He will pay back what he has given. (Proverbs 19:17 NKJV)

This truth is so important. When we give to the poor with right motives—with faith that works by love—we may be giving to the poor, but we are *lending to the Lord.* Clearly, the Bible guarantees that what we have lent to the Lord, He will pay back to us. I can truly testify, on the basis of both observation and personal experience, that the Lord pays very high interest rates on what we lend to Him when we give to the poor. So, always bear this in mind: Helping the poor is lending to the Lord.

"Cast Your Bread upon the Waters"

Then, in Ecclesiastes, we have this advice:

Cast your bread upon the waters, for after many days you will find it again. Give portions to seven, yes to eight, for you do not know what disaster may come upon the land.

(Ecclesiastes 11:1–2)

"Casting our bread upon the waters" is a way ordained in Scripture for us to prepare for possible disaster in the future. It is not the way most people in this world would think of preparing for adversity—but it works. I have seen this principle proven true in my life over and over again. I have done an act of mercy or helped somebody, and then forgotten all about it. Then, ten or twenty years later, God has allowed that bread to come back to me on the waters, and I have received the benefit of what I have given to others.

Ecclesiastes 11:2 says, "*Give portions to seven, yes to eight, for you do not know what disaster may come upon the land.*" *Seven* indicates the fulfillment of all your duties. But *eight* denotes going just a little bit further than duty. In other words, giving to the poor and to others in need is, as it were, paying God's "social security tax."

When you pay your social security to God, that payment is not subject to the depreciation caused by inflation, because there is no inflation in the kingdom of heaven. Furthermore, you will get back what you need, when you need it. For example, if you should become sick or be unable to work due to physical frailty, or if any other situation of need should arise, you can lift your heart to heaven and pray, "Lord, I have given to the poor. I've cast my bread upon the waters. Now I'm in need, and I just remind You of the promises of Your Word." *This is God's social security.*

A Puzzling Parable with a Deep Truth

The benefits of God's social security (investing the way God instructs by giving to the poor and helping others) extend out of time and into eternity. This truth is illustrated by a rather unusual parable that Jesus told His disciples about a manager who cheated his master in order to take care of his own future:

> There was a rich man whose manager was accused of wasting his possessions. So he called him in and asked him, "What is this I hear about you? Give an account of your management, because you cannot be manager any longer." The manager said to himself, "What shall I do now? My master is taking away my job. I'm not strong enough to dig, and I'm ashamed to beg—I know what I'll do so that, when I lose my job here, people will welcome me into their houses." So he called in each one of his master's debtors. He asked the first, "How much do you owe my master?" "Eight hundred gallons of olive oil," he replied. The manager told him, "Take your bill, sit down quickly, and make it four hundred." Then he asked the second, "And how much do you owe?" "A thousand bushels of wheat," he replied. He told him, "Take your bill and make it eight hundred." The master commended the dishonest manager because he had acted shrewdly. For the people of this world are more shrewd in dealing with their own kind than are the people of the light.   (Luke 16:1–8)

Isn't that a strange story? The manager gave away money that was not his own. Why? He did so in order to gain acceptance with people who would welcome him when he no longer had a job. Jesus did not condemn the manager for his dishonesty. On the contrary, He commended him for his shrewdness and told His disciples that they needed to learn the lesson of this parable.

What is its lesson? *That we need to give away money that will make us "friends."* (See Luke 16:9.) Jesus said that if we do so, when we are no longer able to take care of ourselves, the friends we have made with our money will welcome us into eternal homes.

This is a beautiful truth, if only we can grasp it. First, if you are a child of God, your money is not really your own. You are just a steward of it—a manager of God's money. Jesus declared that it is acceptable in God's kingdom to give God's money away to people by investing in the kingdom. Then, when you have come to the end of your life, the people you have invested in—the missionaries you have supported, the souls who have been saved through your giving to various Christian causes, and so on—will be there in eternity, waiting for you. They will be saying things such as this: "Thank you for the hundred dollars you sent to that missionary. As a result of that money you gave, I was saved. I have an eternal home in heaven. I want to invite you to come into my home."

If you are a child of God, your money is not really your own. You are just a steward of it— a manager of God's money.

Although the above is a strange parable, it has such deep meaning. I look back with great satisfaction on the money I have been able to invest over the years, by the grace of God, in different ministries that have brought souls into the kingdom of heaven. One day, when I myself have come to the end of my life, and I step out of time into eternity, the people to whom I have given God's money will welcome me into eternal homes.

This truth is just one additional aspect of what we have termed "God's social security." In the next chapter, we will look at another aspect of security from God that comes from doing His will.

23

SECURITY THROUGH DOING GOD'S WILL

Let us now focus on a very special kind of security that covers every area of our lives. It is the security that comes from doing God's will. We read about this type of security at the end of the following passage:

> For all that is in the world, the lust of the flesh and the lust of the eyes and the boastful pride of life, is not from the Father, but is from the world. The world is passing away, and also its lusts; but the one who does the will of God lives forever.
>
> (1 John 2:16–17 NASB)

United with God's Will

Throughout this study on security, the Bible has consistently been reminding us that there are two different realms of life. The Scriptures contrast the temporal realm (the realm of the earthly, temporary, impermanent, and insecure) with the eternal realm (the realm of God and His permanent, unending kingdom). We see that contrast clearly in the above passage.

Speaking about *"all that is in the world,"* John listed three kinds of motivations that drive people: *"the lust of the flesh and the lust of the eyes and the boastful pride of life."* John wrote that these kinds of motivations are *"not from the Father, but...from the world."*

Furthermore, he declared that *"the world is passing away."* The world is temporary; it will not last. Accordingly, it does not and cannot offer permanent security.

Contrasted with the impermanence of this world is another type of security that John expressed in this way: *"The one who does the will of God lives forever."* What a tremendous statement! If you are doing the will of God, you will live forever. That means that you will never ultimately be overthrown; your security will never be taken from you, and nothing will ever be able to overcome or hinder you.

When you set your heart, mind, and will to do the will of God, you unite with His will. In the final analysis, the will of God is going to prevail over all other forces in the universe. And, if you are united with the will of God by your decision and commitment, then you are going to prevail along with His will. God's strength is going to become yours, because you are doing His will.

Jesus Shows the Way

Jesus is our pattern in His motivation to do the will of God. He said, *"I have come down from heaven not to do my will but to do the will of him who sent me"* (John 6:38). Jesus' entire motivation was to do the will of God the Father. There is an interesting instance in the ministry of Jesus that demonstrates how this worked in His life. In John 4, Jesus was resting by the well of Jacob in Samaria. His disciples had gone to the nearest town to buy food, which they evidently needed for their journey. While they were gone, a Samaritan woman came along. To sum up what happened: Jesus spoke to her about the water of eternal life, and the woman came to some kind of faith in Jesus.

Shortly thereafter, Jesus' disciples came back with the food they had bought. This is what happened next:

> *Meanwhile his disciples urged him, "Rabbi, eat something."*
> *But he said to them, "I have food to eat that you know nothing*

about." Then his disciples said to each other, "Could someone have brought him food?" "My food," said Jesus, "is to do the will of him who sent me and to finish his work."

(John 4:31–34)

The disciples were amazed. They knew that when they had left to go into the town, Jesus had been hungry and in need of food. But now that they had returned with the food, He did not need to eat it. Where had He gotten food? Jesus gave them this remarkable answer: *"My food…is to do the will of him who sent me* [God the Father] *and to finish his work."*

What does physical food mean to us? It is our source of bodily strength and support. But Jesus said, in effect, "I have another source of nourishment that is not mere natural food. It is to do the will of God My Father. And when I do His will, that supplies Me with strength and vitality." You see, in doing God's will, Jesus was *absolutely secure.*

Jesus' entire motivation was to do the will of God the Father.

Irresistible in the Will of God

In various places in the Gospels, we read how Jesus' enemies tried to kill Him (before He was ultimately arrested and put to death on the cross). But they were unable to do so because it was not the will of God for Him to die in that way or at that time. For instance, in the book of John, we read, *"They* [His enemies] *tried to seize him, but no one laid a hand on him, because his time had not yet come"* (John 7:30).

Jesus was not protected by a personal armed security force. To the natural eye, He was absolutely vulnerable. Yet no one could touch Him, because His time had not yet come. By being committed to do the will of God until that will was fulfilled in His life, Jesus was irresistible. How so? In the sense that His opponents were unable to resist Him as He moved forward in God's plan.

The book of Luke records the following incident, which occurred in Jesus' hometown of Nazareth after He had spoken to the people in the synagogue and angered them by what He said:

> *All the people in the synagogue were furious when they heard this. They got up, drove him out of the town, and took him to the brow of the hill on which the town was built, in order to throw him down the cliff. But he walked right through the crowd and went on his way.* (Luke 4:28–30)

Again, Jesus did not have a human security force. Yet there was something about Him that made Him irresistible—unstoppable in the will of God. No one could lay hands on Him, and no one could destroy Him. Why? Once more, because He was committed to do the will of God. And until the will of God was fulfilled in His life, He could not be resisted.

Contrast the above incident at Nazareth with the scene in the garden of Gethsemane when the time had come for Jesus to be taken away and crucified. When the soldiers came to arrest Him, Jesus said,

> *The hour has come; behold, the Son of Man is being betrayed into the hands of sinners.* (Mark 14:41 NASB)

This betrayal and arrest could not have happened before the hour appointed by God the Father. Until that moment, Jesus was absolutely irresistible.

Equally Committed, Equally Irresistible

You and I can follow the pattern Jesus set in this regard. We can be equally invincible, or irresistible, if we are totally committed to, and united with, the will of God. If our motivation is to do God's will, then we are as secure, as strong, and as irresistible in this world as the will of God the Father Himself.

It is important to understand that each one of us can be as committed to do God's will as Jesus was. Psalm 40:7–8 is a prophetic picture of Jesus that is quoted about Him in Hebrews 10:7. However, this picture need not be a depiction of Jesus alone. If we will make the same decision and the same commitment, it can be a picture of each one of us, as well.

> Then I said, "Here I am, I have come—it is written about me in the scroll. I desire to do your will, O my God; your law is within my heart." (Psalm 40:7–8)

The writer of Hebrews explained that those words were fulfilled in Jesus. (See Hebrews 10:5–10.) In Psalm 40, Jesus was saying, prophetically, "Here I am, I have come—it is written about me in the scroll." The "scroll" is the prophetic record of Scripture revealing the will of God in the course of Jesus' life. His work, His destiny, and what was appointed for Him to do had all been set out for Him—and His purpose was to fulfill what had been written.

In a certain sense, this is like an actor in a play who has a part written for him in the script and whose responsibility it is to play that part. He does not need to think up his own lines or improvise; he is merely to express what the playwright has written as his part. The more perfectly the actor captures his part, the better an actor he is.

This is an illustration of what it means to do the will of God. Our "scenario" is already written for us, although we have to discover it. Paul wrote, "For we are God's workmanship, created in Christ Jesus to do good works, which God prepared in advance for us to do" (Ephesians 2:10). This verse describes the will of God for us. It is a scenario that is already prepared—not something to be improvised as we go through life.

Each one of us can be as committed to
do God's will as Jesus was.

A Part Written for Your Life

I want you to understand that, in the scroll of God's eternal book, there is a part written for your life. Your response should be to confess, like Jesus, "Lord, here I am. I have come to You, and I am committed to You. My whole purpose in life is to do what is written about me in the scroll of Your book."

When you live your life with that intent, you are just as invincible and invulnerable as Jesus Himself was. No one could touch Him or stop Him, as long as He was walking out the part that had been written for Him in God's script.

It is so important that you see this truth! You are God's new creation in Christ, and He has chosen you to do something specific and significant to fulfill His plan in your generation. True security in this life comes from committing yourself to God, finding the role He has for you, and then carrying it out.

Would you like to respond to this opportunity for security right now? You can, with the simple prayer we looked at above. Here is what you can confess in response to the pattern Jesus has set for us:

Lord, here I am. I have come to You, and I am committed to You. My whole purpose in life is to do what is written about me in the scroll of Your book. Amen.

24

HOW TO BE "IRRESISTIBLE"

Let us continue to explore the nature of the security that comes from fulfilling God's will in our lives. I want to illustrate the same principle of "irresistibility" using an account from the life of Joshua, one of God's servants in the Old Testament. In considering Joshua's life, please absorb the fact that you can be irresistible, as well, if you will apply the principles outlined in this chapter.

Commissioned to Serve

Joshua had spent forty years in the wilderness serving Moses and being prepared to become a leader. When Moses died, Joshua—as God's appointed successor—took over the leadership of Israel. These are the words with which God commissioned him:

*Moses my servant is dead. Now then, you and all these people, get ready to cross the Jordan River into the land I am about to give to them—to the Israelites. I will give you every place where you set your foot, as I promised Moses. Your territory will extend from the desert to Lebanon, and from the great river, the Euphrates—all the Hittite country—to the Great Sea on the west. **No one will be able to stand up against you all the days of your life.** As I was with Moses, so I will be with you; I will never leave you nor forsake you. Be strong* *and courageous, because you will lead these people to inherit the land I swore to their forefathers to give them. Be strong and very courageous. Be careful to obey all the law my servant Moses gave you; do not turn from it to the right or to the left, **that you may be successful wherever you go.** Do not let this Book of the Law depart from your mouth; meditate on it day and night, so that you may be careful to do everything written in it. Then you will be prosperous and successful. Have not I commanded you? Be strong and courageous. Do not be terrified; do not be discouraged, for the* LORD *your God will be with you wherever you go.*   (Joshua 1:2–9)

That was Joshua's commission, given to him personally by the Lord.

Features of the Commission

There are some important features of the commission that are relevant to our lives today. The first is Joshua's God-given assignment: *"You will lead these people to inherit the land"* (Joshua 1:6). In the previous chapter, we saw that there is a scroll in God's book that has an assignment for each one of us—a part to play in God's eternal plan. Joshua's role was to lead the Israelites into the Promised Land. We must therefore begin with this fact: *We have an assignment.* That is the basis for our security.

Second, we see that Joshua had a special source of strength that was dependent upon God's Word. *"Do not let this Book of the Law depart from your mouth; meditate on it day and night, so that you may be careful to do everything written in it"* (Joshua 1:8).

I have often interpreted this verse in the following way: *"Think the law, speak the law, act on the law."* God's Word is available to us, and the same principles apply exactly to us as they applied to

Joshua. We must *think* God's Word; we do so by meditating on it. Then, we must *speak* God's Word; the power of His Word has to be in our mouths. Finally, we must *act on* God's Word; we must "*do everything written in it*," or obey it. These are the basic requirements.

Third, on the basis of this commission to depend upon God's Word, Joshua was again told to "*be strong and courageous*" (Joshua 1:9). Note that in verses 6, 7, and 9, the Lord gave the same admonishment to Joshua—three times altogether.

When God tells us to be strong and courageous, it is very encouraging and wonderful. We may rejoice, saying, "God has told me to be strong and courageous!" However, let me tell you something you need to know: God always tells us to be strong and courageous for a good reason! What is that reason? We are going to be in a situation where we are going to *need* strength and courage. So, while this command is encouraging, it is also a kind of warning. Just as Joshua needed to be strong and courageous to fulfill his God-given assignment, we also, in order to fulfill our God-given assignment, are going to have to be strong and courageous.

Finally, please note God's promise to Joshua that, if he obeyed, God would be with him everywhere. God guaranteed His own personal presence with Joshua all the way through. He promised, "*As I was with Moses, so I will be with you; I will never leave you nor forsake you*" (Joshua 1:5). And again: "*The LORD your God will be with you wherever you go*" (Joshua 1:9).

This promise is for us, also. If we meet God's conditions, He says, "I will be with you all the way. I'll never leave you nor forsake you." When all this has been established in our lives, *we become irresistible*. Joshua was irresistible, as we read in Joshua 1:5: "*No one will be able to stand up against you all the days of your life.*"

Here is the important condition: The above is true for you only if you are walking in the will of God. If you are walking in the will of God, then anyone or anything that opposes you is actually opposing God. If you step out of God's will, you lose that irresistibility. However, while you are in the will of God—walking out your God-given assignment; thinking, speaking, and acting on the Word of God; walking in obedience and total commitment—then this promise of God is just as true for you as it was for Joshua: *"No one will be able to stand up against you all the days of your life."*

We have an assignment—that is the basis for our security.

A Pattern of Principles

Let us now review the commission of Joshua as a pattern for us, so we will be sure to apply in our own lives the principles the Lord laid down for him. Let me suggest that there are three requirements we need to bear in mind, all of which are illustrated very clearly in Joshua's experience.

First, we must base our lives on God's Word. That was God's instruction to Joshua: *"Do not let this Book of the Law depart from your mouth; meditate on it day and night, so that you may be careful to do everything written in it"* (Joshua 1:8). Again, in summary, we must *think* the Word of God, *speak* the Word of God, and *act on* the Word of God.

Second, we must be strong and courageous. God has made provision for us to be strong and courageous—it is the provision of the Holy Spirit. Paul said to his disciple Timothy, *"God did not give us a spirit of timidity, but a spirit of power, of love and of self-discipline"* (2 Timothy 1:7). If we walk in the power of Holy Spirit, filled with the Holy Spirit, He excludes timidity, because there is no room for it. As we discussed in chapter 18, the Holy Spirit is the Spirit *"of power, of love and of self-discipline."*

Third, we must advance and not retreat. *We cannot go back; we must go forward.* We should never focus on self-protection or self-preservation. We must focus on moving ahead in the will of God.

Jesus' Authority Is Our Security

The following is the commission Jesus gave to His disciples:

All authority in heaven and on earth has been given to me. Therefore go and make disciples of all nations, baptizing them in the name of the Father and of the Son and of the Holy Spirit, and teaching them to obey everything I have commanded you. And surely I am with you always, to the very end of the age.
(Matthew 28:18–20)

The fact that *"all authority"* has been given to Jesus as the King of Kings and Lord of Lords is not only the basis of His commission, but it is also the source of the disciples' security. Exactly the same promise is given to you and me—if we go in obedience to Jesus' commission, setting our faces to do the will of God. When we do so, we will not focus on self-protection or self-preservation. We will not be afraid. We will not retreat.

Joshua's assignment was to lead the Israelites into the Promised Land; our assignment is to take the gospel of the kingdom to all nations of the world. Undergirding us is the authority of Jesus Himself. From His heavenly throne, He overshadows us, protects us, and provides for us. He has promised to walk with us, making us irresistible, if we go in obedience to His commission.

25

SECURITY IN ADVERSITY

In this final chapter, we will explore the principle of irresistibility as it was demonstrated in the life and ministry of a great servant of God in the New Testament—the apostle Paul. We will observe how he withstood adversity. We will examine what Paul experienced toward the end of his life, at a time when, in the natural, everything had gone wrong—people had deserted and opposed him, and he was lacking items that were very precious to him.

Without seeming pessimistic, I want to tell you that, sooner or later, you are going to find yourself in a situation of adversity. It may not be exactly the same kind of situation that Paul faced. But, at one time or another, you are going to be confronted with trials. And, when adversity comes, you must be sure to have the kind of security that does not desert you in the midst of your troubles—a security that sees you through the lonely place, the difficult place, the hard place.

Paul's Adversity

Let us look at the portrait of Paul found in his second letter to his disciple Timothy. From a human perspective, it seems that at this point in the apostle's life, everything was against him. He was in a Roman jail awaiting trial by one of the most wicked and corrupt rulers in human history—the emperor Nero. Paul was almost certain that he would be condemned to execution. He was now an elderly man, and perhaps his strength was failing. It was cold in the jail, and he did not have adequate clothing. Just about everything that could be against a person was against Paul. Beyond these adversities, he was left alone without his fellow workers. Here is what he wrote to Timothy from prison:

> Do your best to come to me quickly, for Demas, because he loved this world, has deserted me and has gone to Thessalonica. Crescens has gone to Galatia, and Titus to Dalmatia. Only Luke is with me....Erastus stayed in Corinth, and I left Trophimus sick in Miletus.   (2 Timothy 4:9–11, 20)

Abandoned and Opposed

In his letter, Paul stated that Demas, one of Paul's closest friends and trusted associates, had gone back on his commitment—not only to Paul but also to Christ. Then Paul listed others who were no longer there to encourage him: Crescens, Titus, and Erastus. Finally, he wrote that he had to leave Trophimus sick in Miletus, which was another bitter disappointment to him. Even the great apostle Paul apparently did not get his prayers answered for Trophimus, and he ended up having to leave his fellow worker in the care of others.

In addition, Paul had been harmed by his enemies. He seems not to have harbored any bitterness against them, but the experience was nonetheless an objective reality for him. He wrote,

> Alexander the metalworker did me a great deal of harm. The Lord will repay him for what he has done. You too should be on your guard against him, because he strongly opposed our message. At my first defense, no one came to my support, but everyone deserted me. May it not be held against them.
> (2 Timothy 4:14–16)

It will do us well to note again that this passage contains no vindictiveness or bitterness toward his enemies; Paul left his situation in the Lord's hands. And, beyond the opposition of his enemies, he said of his friends, *"Everyone deserted me."*

Facing Physical Discomfort

In addition, as I wrote earlier, Paul was without adequate clothing—and equipment. He wrote to Timothy, *"When you come, bring the cloak that I left with Carpus at Troas, and my scrolls, especially the parchments"* (2 Timothy 4:13).

When I read the words *"bring the cloak,"* I see Paul in that stone dungeon with winter coming on and no warm clothing at hand. He was human like the rest of us and susceptible to physical discomfort. Personally, one of the weather conditions that is most difficult for me to endure is cold. When I read in 2 Corinthians 11:27 that Paul suffered cold and nakedness, I shudder inside. But there he was in that prison cell without sufficient clothing or provision for the cold, with winter approaching.

Why did Paul want the scrolls, *"especially the parchments"*? I believe he wanted to write letters, and he did not have the material to do so. I do not think he intended to write letters to complain about his situation. Rather than being focused on himself, I think he was concerned for the Christian churches and the disciples he knew in various parts of the ancient world. He longed to comfort and encourage them.

Finishing His Course

So, the above is our picture of Paul at the end of his life in a situation of extreme adversity. What was Paul's attitude in the midst of this circumstance? He stated it himself:

> *I am already being poured out like a drink offering, and the time has come for my departure. I have fought the good fight, I have finished the race, I have kept the faith.*
>
> (2 Timothy 4:6–7)

We need to understand the image Paul used here. In the Old Testament, with every animal that was offered in sacrifice, a drink offering of wine was also offered. The sacrifice of the animal was not complete without the drink offering. Paul was saying, "I have offered to the Lord the sacrifice of my labors—the disciples I have made, the churches I have founded—but to make that sacrifice complete, my own life is being poured out like a drink offering."

I have found from personal experience that if you are going to keep the faith, you have to fight the fight. Faith is a fight. It takes courage. It takes determination. It takes commitment. In spite of the adversity, Paul said, "'I have finished the race'; I have done all that was allotted to me to do."

Then Paul looked forward—out of time and into eternity. It was as if a window opened in that cell, and he looked beyond those gray stone walls into a different scene.

> *Now there is in store for me the crown of righteousness, which the Lord, the righteous Judge, will award to me on that day— and not only to me, but also to all who have longed for his appearing.* (2 Timothy 4:8)

This statement always touches me, because Paul knew he was soon going to stand before an unrighteous earthly judge who would pronounce an unrighteous sentence against him—a death sentence. In light of what he was facing, he confessed, "This is not the final judgment. There's another one lying ahead. In eternity, I'm going to stand before an absolutely righteous Judge, and He will give me the due reward for all that I have done in His service."

Faith is a fight. It takes courage.
It takes determination. It takes commitment.

Serenity and Security

Paul had such serene confidence. He knew that everything was under God's control; therefore, he had no bitterness and no regrets. What was the secret to Paul's attitude? I believe it was stated beautifully a little earlier in 2 Timothy where, speaking about all that he had been through, Paul said,

> Yet I am not ashamed, because I know whom I have believed, and am convinced that he is able to guard what I have entrusted to him for that day.   (2 Timothy 1:12)

Two key phrases in Paul's statement are the secret to all serenity and security in the face of any situation of adversity.

First, *"I know whom I have believed."* Please note that Paul did not say, "I know *what* I have believed." His security was not a doctrine. It was a Person—the person of the Lord Jesus Christ. It is not enough to believe in a doctrine. That doctrine has to take you to the person of the Savior, to the Lord Jesus. Do you know *in whom* you have believed?

The second key phrase is, *"I...am convinced that he is able to guard what I have entrusted to him."* The King James Version reads, *"...that which I have committed unto him."* That is the secret to true security. It is total commitment to God and to His will. When you have committed your life—all that you have, all that you are, and all that you are ever going to be—into the hands of God, you can be absolutely sure that He is able to guard what you have entrusted to Him.

Let us end this book with that commitment, which we have identified as the secret to true security. Will you pray with me?

Dear Lord, I praise You and thank You for being the only real Source of security in this life and for eternity. I affirm this truth by totally committing my life to You now. All that I have, all that I am, and all that I will ever be, I place in Your hands, knowing and proclaiming that You alone are able to guard and keep everything I am entrusting to You.

Lord, I again acknowledge that You alone are my total security in this life and the next, and I surrender myself completely into Your hands. Amen.

ABOUT THE AUTHOR

Derek Prince (1915–2003) was born in Bangalore, India, into a British military family. He was educated as a scholar of classical languages at Eton College and Cambridge University in England and later at Hebrew University, Israel. As a student, he was a philosopher and self-proclaimed agnostic.

While in the British Medical Corps during World War II, Prince began to study the Bible as a philosophical work. Converted through a powerful encounter with Jesus Christ, he was baptized in the Holy Spirit a few days later. This life-changing experience altered the whole course of his life, which he thereafter devoted to studying and teaching the Bible as the Word of God.

Internationally recognized as a Bible scholar and spiritual patriarch, Derek Prince taught and ministered on six continents for more than sixty years. Until a few years before his death at the age of eighty-eight, he traveled the world, imparting God's revealed truth, praying for the sick and afflicted, and sharing his prophetic insights into world events in the light of Scripture. He wrote over fifty books, which have been translated into over one hundred languages and distributed worldwide. He pioneered teaching on such groundbreaking themes as generational curses, the biblical significance of Israel, and demonology.

Derek Prince Ministries, with its international headquarters in Charlotte, North Carolina, continues to distribute his teachings and to train missionaries, church leaders, and congregations through its worldwide national offices. It is estimated that Derek Prince's clear teaching of the Bible has reached more than half the globe through his books, tapes, and daily radio program, which is now known as *Derek Prince Legacy Radio*. In 2002, he said, "It is my desire—and I believe the Lord's desire—that this ministry continue the work which God began through me over sixty years ago, until Jesus returns."